Cambridge Elements

Elements in Politics and Society in Southeast Asia
edited by
Edward Aspinall
Australian National University
Meredith L. Weiss
University at Albany, SUNY

COURTS AND POLITICS IN SOUTHEAST ASIA

Björn Dressel
Australian National University

CAMBRIDGE
UNIVERSITY PRESS

Shaftesbury Road, Cambridge CB2 8EA, United Kingdom

One Liberty Plaza, 20th Floor, New York, NY 10006, USA

477 Williamstown Road, Port Melbourne, VIC 3207, Australia

314–321, 3rd Floor, Plot 3, Splendor Forum, Jasola District Centre, New Delhi – 110025, India

103 Penang Road, #05–06/07, Visioncrest Commercial, Singapore 238467

Cambridge University Press is part of Cambridge University Press & Assessment, a department of the University of Cambridge.

We share the University's mission to contribute to society through the pursuit of education, learning and research at the highest international levels of excellence.

www.cambridge.org
Information on this title: www.cambridge.org/9781009517737

DOI: 10.1017/9781108770088

First published 2024

A catalogue record for this publication is available from the British Library.

ISBN 978-1-009-51773-7 Hardback
ISBN 978-1-108-72579-8 Paperback
ISSN 2515-2998 (online)
ISSN 2515-298X (print)

Courts and Politics in Southeast Asia

Elements in Politics and Society in Southeast Asia

DOI: 10.1017/9781108770088
First published online: March 2024

Björn Dressel
Australian National University

Author for correspondence: Björn Dressel, bjoern.dressel@anu.edu.au

Abstract: Courts around the globe have become central players in governance, those in Southeast Asia have been no exception. This Element analyses the historical foundations, patterns, and drivers of judicialization of politics by mapping critical junctures that have shaped the emergence of modern courts in the region and providing a basic typology of courts and politics that extends the analysis to the contemporary situation. It also offers a new relational theory that helps explain the dynamics of judicial recruitment, decision-making, court performance—and ultimately perceptions of judicial legitimacy. In a region where power is often concentrated among oligarchs and clientelist political dynamics persist, it posits that courts are best comprehended as institutional hybrids. These hybrids seamlessly blend formal and informal practices, with profound implications for how Southeast Asian courts are molding both the rule of law and political governance.

Keywords: high courts, judicial behavior, rule of law, networks, Southeast Asia

ISBNs: 9781009517737 (HB), 9781108725798 (PB), 9781108770088 (OC)
ISSNs: 2515-2998 (online), 2515-298X (print)

Contents

1 Introduction

Over the last three decades, courts in Southeast Asia have become major players in governance. The regular involvement of the Supreme Court of the Philippines in the country's volatile politics was long considered exceptional in the region, but not anymore. Consider the role of courts in Thailand's continuing political turmoil or the intervention of courts in high-profile religious and political cases in Malaysia and Indonesia. Even in authoritarian and semi-authoritarian settings like Vietnam, Cambodia, Myanmar, or Singapore, there are occasional signs of greater judicial assertiveness considering that the primacy of law over politics remains deeply contested.

Hirschl (2006, 721) described this trend toward the judicialization of politics as "the ever-accelerating reliance on courts and judicial means for addressing core moral predicaments, public policy questions, and political controversies." Judicialization is particularly crucial in "megapolitical cases," which he defines as those cases that go beyond issues of procedural justice and political salience to include "core political controversies that define (and often divide) whole polities" (Hirschl 2006, 725). This is highlighted in the involvement of judges in core controversies related to executive branch prerogatives, regime transitions, restorative justice, and electoral matters.

The trend has been well-documented in the United States, Europe, and Latin America (see Tate and Vallinder 1995; Epp 1998; Feeley and Rubin 1998; Stone Sweet 2000; Shapiro and Stone Sweet 2002; Sieder, Schjolden, and Angell 2005b). Its emergence in Asia, particularly Southeast Asia, has been largely unexplored and, thus, limits the understanding of the role of courts in politics in the region and what such understanding might contribute to the field of comparative judicial politics globally (for tentative exploration see Ginsburg and Chen 2009; Harding and Nicholson 2010; Dressel 2012).

This lacuna in scholarship is unsurprising: The region still battles traditional executive dominance, questionable rule of law, and an unusual degree of regime diversity – all of which have higher visibility than what is happening in the courts themselves. Almost thirty years ago with many regimes neither democratic nor constitutional, a leading scholar claimed that "a majority of Southeast Asian countries are unlikely candidates for the judicialization of politics" (Tate 1994, 188).

Much has changed in the interim. In most states, as political and economic liberalization has advanced (albeit not always in a linear way), many countries have become more concerned about the rule of law as well as accountability and rights issues. Promoting the rule of law has gained considerable traction as new democracies emerging from authoritarian rule consolidate recent democratic gains. Democratizing countries see the courts as central to addressing previous injustice and promoting socioeconomic rights. Meanwhile many less liberal regimes have also chosen constitutional and judicial reform to tighten social control, enhance legitimacy, and ensure credible policy outcomes (Ginsburg and Moustafa 2008). Therefore, courts have become central to political life in many countries.

The spread of judicial review, the continuing professionalization of lawyers, and other institutional changes have been major drivers of this trend (see Section 2). As shown in Table 1, all but two states in Southeast Asia have established judicial review and strengthened the courts, sometimes through constitutional, administrative, and other specialized courts.

These developments have been supported by conventional wisdom from the policy community that an empowered judiciary is a force for stable – if not necessarily "good" – governance. Reform advocates and academics generally see courts as critical to upholding the rule of law by protecting basic rights and freedoms and ensuring that commitments of state actors in areas such as property rights are credible. They also assume that courts give citizens stability and security when their interpretation of laws mitigates societal conflict. They are thought to hold government actors accountable and provide political checks and balances, thus limiting and making the government more responsive. In short, by promoting the rule of law, hemming in government, and gradually judicializing governance, judges are seen as critical to rule-based constitutional governance (Shapiro 1981; Feeley and Rubin 1998; Haggard, MacIntyre, and Tiede 2008).

A closer look at the state of courts and politics in Southeast Asia, however, reveals that reality can be very different from common assumptions. To begin with, the variation in the patterns of judicial behavior in the region demands that attention be given to the nuances of the judicialization trend. Greater judicial assertiveness – ostensibly to promote the rule of law, and make governments more accountable, responsive, and stable – has had ambiguous effects. Some courts have actively intervened in politics to enhance constitutional practice by checking executive abuse, upholding the supremacy of law, and protecting the rights of citizens (e.g., the Philippines, Indonesia). Others, however, have subverted the rule of law and actively undermined mechanisms of accountability in favor of narrow interests (e.g., Thailand, Cambodia). Still, others have been deliberately muted or self-restrained when engaging with core issues of political governance, which raises concerns about their autonomy and independence (e.g., Singapore, Malaysia, Myanmar).

The degree of regime diversity in the region might partly explain these patterns but what is striking are the differences between states with similar

Table 1 Judicial review in Southeast Asia

Country	First Constitution (Last Major Amendment)	Freedom House Ranking (2020)	Type of Review (CR=Constitutional; JR=Judicial)	Reviewing Institution (Year Established)
Brunei	1959 (2004)	28/100 (not free)	No review, only interpretation	Interpretation Tribunal (1984)
Cambodia	1947 (1999)	25/100 (not free)	CR	Constitutional Council (1993)
Indonesia	1945 (1999, 2000, 2001, 2002)	61/100 (partly free)	CR	Constitutional Court (1997)
Laos	1947 (2015)	14/100 (not free)	CR	National Assembly Standing Committee (2015)
Malaysia	1957 (*)	52/100 (partly free)	JR	High Court (1957)
Myanmar	1947 (2008)	30/100 (partly free)	CR	Constitutional Tribunal (2008)
The Philippines	1898 (1986)	59/100 (partly free)	JR	Supreme Court (1987)

Table 1 (cont.)

Country	First Constitution (Last Major Amendment)	Freedom House Ranking (2020)	Type of Review (CR=Constitutional; JR=Judicial)	Reviewing Institution (Year Established)
Singapore	1959 (*)	50/100 (partly free)	JR	High Court (1969)
Thailand	1932 (1997, 2008, 2017)	32/100 (partly free)	CR	Constitutional Court (1998)
Timor-Leste	2002	71/100 (free)	JR	Supreme Court (N/A)
Vietnam	1946 (2001, 2013)	20/100 (not free)	No review, only supervision	National Assembly

Source: Hill and Menzel (2002), Tan (2002), Chang et al. 2014, 132; Freedom House scores (https://freedomhouse.org/countries/freedom-world/scores), (author compilation).

Note: *Constant revision.

institutions and political environments. Developments in Southeast Asia raise a variety of theoretical and empirical questions related to the study of courts and politics in the region, most notably: What forces shape judicial politics in the region and how can we systematize our understanding of the patterns we observe there? What features can help us understand variations in judicial behavior and how well do they account for realities in the region? Finally, when does greater judicial empowerment reinforce or support a move toward liberal constitutional governance, and when does it lead to other political patterns?

1.1 Views from the Literature

Confronted with these challenges from the region and seeking answers to some of these questions, scholarship has largely fallen into two camps: legal and political. Although it is the latter that has engaged most fruitfully with judicial behavior, both are considered complementary rather than mutually exclusive as each camp has a distinct focus.

Legal scholars, particularly those working on comparative constitutional law, have traditionally tracked developments in the jurisprudence of high courts and engaged in normative questions emerging from the application of the law. This has meant prolific engagement with country-specific developments in jurisprudence, legal doctrine, and areas of professional ethics (e.g., Butt 2015; Lee and Pittard 2017a; Tew 2020). Nevertheless, similar regional developments across Southeast Asia's diverse landscape have also prompted a growing comparative engagement with the changing institutional landscape of courts as part of empirical studies, including constitutional changes, the establishment of specialized courts, gender dynamics in the judiciary, and shared legal developments in areas of judicial review, rights and liberties, and constitutional culture (Harding and Nicholson 2010; Chen 2018; Chen and Harding 2018; Crouch 2021).

Meanwhile, sociolegal scholars have engaged in normative and conceptual discussions of the rule of law. This includes highlighting differences in how judicial and political actors in the region understand the rule of law and the very different realities of how justice institutions and processes function (Engel and Engel 2010; McCargo 2020). This has led to a much broader critical engagement with global rule of law debates (Tamahana 2004; Krygier 2016). This includes nuances in how the rule of law plays out in light of the region's diverse legal history and cultural, political, and legal systems as expressed in thin (procedural) vs. thick (substantial) notions, or the closely related concepts of rule of law vs. rule by law (Peerenboom 2004; Rajah 2012; Hurst 2020), and law and order (Cheesman 2015).

The rule of law literature touches on debates on authoritarian resilience, constitutional backsliding, and authoritarian legalism in the region that have brought back a concern with the role of judicial institutions in facilitating (and/or resisting) this process (Ginsburg and Moustafa 2008; Rajah 2012). Taken together, the legal literature has contributed to a general acknowledgment of the rich tapestry of legal developments in the region. Despite increasing points of convergence in terms of judicial and legal institutions, there remains considerable diversity in actual practice between states in the region (Chen 2010; Chang et al. 2014; Yap 2017; Lee and Pittard 2017b). Nevertheless, the focus of the rule of law literature has not been on the courts and even less so on judicial behavior.

Filling this void, scholars of comparative judicial politics have drawn attention to the courts and judicial behavior, asking three central questions:

1. Why are countries in the region adopting judicial review?
2. Under what conditions do courts exert these powers assertively and successfully?
3. Now that their powers have been expanded, how do judges decide cases as they do? Other than independent judgment on how the law applies to the facts before them, what forces are likely to influence their decisions?

Answers to these questions have prompted vivid debates, especially since countries in the region seem to evade simple classification. Grappling with how to structure court review of the constitutional validity of legislative and executive acts, scholars have drawn on strategic-rational accounts to explain the establishment of judicial review in the region and elsewhere. For instance, the *electoral* or *insurance* model views judicial review as strategic insurance by elites against political uncertainty. It implies that fragmentation of the political system, as measured by the competitiveness of political parties, is a critical driver of the choice of judicial review and it ultimately shapes the independence and related performance of judges (Ginsburg 2003).

Alternatively, the *hegemonic preservation* theory views judicial review and the resulting empowerment of courts as the "by-product of a strategic interplay" between influential socio-political groups (e.g., politicians, economic elites, and judges themselves) that insulates challenged policy preferences against popular pressure (Hirschl 2004, 43). Applying such view, scholars trying to make sense of constitutional and judicial developments in Thailand have shown how the judicialization trend is driven primarily by the strategic motivations of political elites (Dressel 2010; Mérieau 2016). Nonetheless, experiences in other countries have underscored the importance of legal mobilization by civil society and legal actors in initiating court cases, as this plays a vital role in engaging the judiciary in a form of "judicialization from below" (Epp 1998).

The second central question is concerned with the conditions under which courts exert their judicial review powers successfully. This question is common among scholars puzzled by the diversity of court behavior in the region, particularly in high-profile political cases. In an attempt to explain the waxing and waning of assertive behavior of courts over time, scholars have conducted typological work on court behavior through multicountry comparative and paired comparisons (e.g., Croissant 2010; Lin 2017), and in-depth studies of single cases (e.g., Pompe 2005; Lin 2009; Ciencia Jr. 2012; Kanagasabai 2012; Johnson 2016).

Scholars have also emphasized structural factors, such as whether the political regime is authoritarian or democratic (Yap 2017); the political and legal powers that courts have been assigned; how much the legal complex and the public support a court (Deinla 2014); and the structure of local political elites (Dressel and Mietzner 2012; Tonsakulrungruang 2017). Finally, attention has been drawn to internal court dynamics, such as how court leaders interact (Hendrianto 2018) or evolving values and preferences on the bench (Panthip and Garoupa 2016).

All this work fails to point to a single comprehensive theory and instead recognizes that the behavior of judges and the assertive exercise of judicial review at critical junctures may be the result of a complex interplay of configurations. As a result, the final question that is increasingly at the center of current regional debates on judicial politics is how to explain the behavior of individual judges on the bench. Once judges are empowered, what might explain how they exercise that power and to what effect? These questions have been at the core of studies of the courts and politics but Southeast Asia has proved to be a difficult terrain for current models.

Traditionally, studies of judicial behavior have been dominated by legalistic, attitudinal, and strategic-rational approaches, which make different assumptions about what motivates and influences a judge's decision (good overview: Segal 2008). Legalistic accounts assume that judges apply the law in conformity with precedent and legal norms; considerations related to the law itself principally guide their behavior; and law and legal mechanisms are the sole limitations on their actions. Attitudinal models downplay the influence of law. They argue that ideological positions and policy preferences shape the decisions of judges and courts, especially in courts of last resort. Finally, the dominant strategic-rational models agree that judges seek to satisfy nonlegal preferences but, in doing so, they must take into account the preferences of other political and institutional actors. Thus, they adapt their preferred outcome to expected responses or to secure the outcomes that will be most acceptable. All the traditional models of judicial behavior assume, although to different degrees, that considerations of policy, particularly legal policy, substantially influences the choices of high courts.

These models have all proved useful elsewhere. But how well do they work in Southeast Asia? Attempts to test for the attitudinal model in the Philippines (Escresa and Garoupa 2012) and Thailand (Pruksacholavit and Garoupa 2016) and to explore judicial ideal points in the Philippines (Pellegrina, Escresa, and Garoupa 2014) have had at best mixed results. So have descriptive statistical explorations of the independence of the voting patterns of justices at the Supreme Court of the Philippines (Desierto 2015), and strategic behavior in high-profile cases in the Malaysian Federal Court (Dressel and Inoue 2022) and the Indonesian Constitutional Court (Dressel and Inoue 2018b). Clearly and unsurprisingly, the region poses fundamental challenges to the core assumptions of current US-derived models of judicial behavior. Political and legal systems in the region are far from solidly institutionalized (legalistic model); ideological and policy preferences are often unobservable (attitudinal model); and strategic responses may at times be informed by nonrational (e.g., emotive, loyalty) dynamics that Western models fail to account for (strategic-rational model).

What emerges from both legal and political studies of the region is, therefore, the need to rethink the factors that shape the relationship between the courts and politics, as highlighted in the growing number of studies from non-Western courts in terms of the historical–institutional foundation for the behavior of judges (Hilbink 2007) or the political context in which law emerged and is applied (Meierhenrich 2010; Massoud 2013). The boundaries between law and politics in the region are often fluid and may sometimes dissolve because of weak institutions and professional practices. What is clear is that both law and politics come into play when judges make decisions, especially in high-profile cases where both act as major constraints (Roux 2018b). Thus, it is critical to ask what type of politics is at play, in what circumstances judges decide based on law and professional considerations, and whether their decisions are based on other extralegal considerations. Such questions matter especially in Asia – a region where courts are still subject to executive and third-party interference, corruption, and informal practices that directly challenge ideals of rule-based governance.

1.2 Rethinking Courts and Politics in Southeast Asia

My goal in this Element is to show that Southeast Asia has much to offer to move these debates forward, especially given the empirical challenges to the theories of judicial behavior and court performance that have traditionally dominated the literature. I provide a novel theoretical argument about how best to understand court dynamics in the region and possibly beyond. It starts by drawing attention to the oligarchic power concentration and clientelist-political dynamics still pervasive in the region. It acknowledges that bureaucratic-state institutions in Southeast Asia, including the courts, are best understood as institutional hybrids in which formal and informal practices are closely interwoven and relational and personal relationships are intrinsic to institutional realities. More specifically, it should be recognized that clientelist patterns breed varying networks that play a role in influencing the judiciary to create distinct patterns of activism, politicization, restraint, and muteness. Competitive-oligarchic settings allow for competing networks to seek influence over the judiciary, driving dissent and propelling greater activism (e.g., the Philippines and Indonesia). This is compounded by institutional empowerment of the courts. By contrast, patronal-clientelist regimes stifle competing networks and allow for the capture of the court by a single network (e.g., Thailand). The degree of hegemonic political structures over time limit the role of competing networks, thereby limiting court activity to a spectrum of muteness to restraint in megapolitical cases (e.g., Malaysia and Singapore). As a result, a concern with formal institutional roles and arrangements seem insufficient for understanding courts and judges. This focus needs to be complemented by an understanding of how informal arrangements and dynamics function within court processes.

As highlighted by a growing number of studies of courts, particularly in Latin America, sub-Saharan Africa, and Asia, judges cannot insulate themselves from informal norms of friendship, clientelism, corruption, and patrimonialism, even as those norms may compete with formal institutions and rules. Thus, identifying dynamic patterns of personal interactions, relations, and identity-based ties on and off the bench can be critical to an understanding of how judges behave and how extensive judicial networks may capture the informal dynamics that might influence a variety of outcomes. Among these dynamics are appointments to the bench, actual independence of courts, court reforms, and judicial decisions (Dressel, Sanchez Urribarri, and Stroh 2018).

Recognizing that lawyers and judges in the region are becoming ever more professionalized, I argue that judges in Southeast Asia must deal with a dynamic tension between relational ties of loyalty, friendship, and clientelistic obligations versus adherence to standards derived from the law itself, as well as with professional expectations generated by local and global expectations. This tension and the extent to which judges, particularly in the highest courts, are able to disentangle themselves from their ever-present relational ties help explain the variability of judicial performance, especially in high-profile constitutional cases.

Because it draws attention to the informal nature of judicial politics, such a perspective appears particularly suitable in Southeast Asia. The region has often been analyzed in terms of how patrimonialism, clientelism, and personalized politics are expressed in political institutions such as the legislature, the executive, or the state at large (e.g., Lande 1983; Hutchcroft 2017; Aspinall and Berenschot 2019). However, these approaches have rarely been applied to the courts, despite studies of courts in the region increasingly addressing deep-rooted cultures of corruption (Dick and Lindsey 2002); executive pressures; influences on court decisions and judicial appointments (Khoo 1999; Chua et al. 2012); and the exercise of broader political connections when courts have become politicized (Dressel and Tonsakulrungruang 2019).

Introducing a novel relational approach to the courts and politics not only resonates with regional dynamics, it also allows for a unique perspective on the three central scholarly concerns about the courts and politics raised here. It invites research into the formation and effects of judges' networks and their political counterparts; how such networks shape the operation and independence of courts in the region and how judges understand their role; and, most challenging, how relationships on and off the bench may influence the opinions of individual judges to possibly produce the patterns that we observe.

With that thesis in mind, the Element is structured as follows: Section 2 provides a historical account of the trajectory of court institutions in the region. Mapping common critical junctures that have shaped the emergence of modern courts in the region, I provide the reader with a description of the hybrid context in which judicial institutions emerged and operate in Southeast Asia and what has driven their gradual acquisition of influence in the region over the last three decades. Section 3 provides a basic typology of judicial politics, illustrated by a description of court dynamics in selected cases to illustrate changes and nuances in the judicialization trend. I introduce a new relational argument to analyze court performance and judicial behavior that recognizes that both are best understood in terms of the clientelist–political dynamics pervasive in the region. Section 4 applies this framework to selected cases in the region, paying particular attention to the involvement of courts in high-profile cases. Section 5 concludes by reflecting on the implications of judicial empowerment for the rule of law and political governance in Southeast Asia and a broader comparative study of judicial institutions and behavior.

2 How Southeast Asia's Courts Evolved

Providing a brief historical account of the courts in Southeast Asia is not easy. At first glance, the countries in this "immensely varied region marked by some notable unities and containing great diversity" (Osborne 2004, 16) seem to have little in common in terms of ethnicity, religion, language, political systems, or economic development – much less legal traditions and institutions. The label "Southeast Asia" itself was merely invented by the British high command for military reasons in World War II to distinguish this diverse geostrategic area from India, China, and the Pacific (Fifield 1983).

However, the subsequent birth of institutions like the Association of Southeast Asian Nations (ASEAN) in 1967 has since helped to consolidate the notion of a geographical and cultural unit that incorporates eleven diverse states. Historians and anthropologists gradually reinforced this identity by describing the many historical interactions and shared trajectories within and between populations in mainland and maritime Southeast Asia – some of which have shaped similar institutional patterns and developments despite the diversity (Steinberg 1988).

The emergence and evolution of courts in the region is a good illustration of shared historical patterns and how trajectories converged in Southeast Asia. Throughout the region, justice institutions were traditionally linked closely to localized personal rule. It is only with the creation of modern centralized states, generally as part of the Western colonial endeavor, that courts as a modern institution have emerged. Thus, despite considerable diversity, judicial institutions within the region have experienced very similar impulses. Many started with colonial state-building and were further consolidated through postcolonial nationalist modernization efforts, and thereafter reinforced by a regional wave of liberalization and democratization at the end of the Cold War. Naturally, however, the process has not evolved in a straight line or without setbacks.

Like the broader process of "institutional layering" of old and new (see Mahoney and Thelen 2010), legal scholars have described the evolution of courts and legal systems in the region generally in terms of "a series of layers, each of which overlays the previous layers without actually replacing them, so that in places, due to tectonic shifts, the lower layers are still visible, although not perfectly distinguishable from each other" (Harding 2001, 205). A different way to describe these dynamics, in line with the argument of this Element, is to view the move toward modern, impersonal justice institutions as often incomplete because these institutions have not managed to disentangle themselves from the traditional, personalized patterns of rule that have been dominant in the region for centuries. Thus, most court systems are really hybrids: institutions that appear modern but continue to be influenced by informal personal relationships despite formal rules in their day-to-day operations. This is notable in the persistent practice of clientelism and patronage permeating judicial institutions.

Before illustrating the argument further through a typology of judicial politics and a new relational approach to judicial behavior (Section 3), I will briefly outline the historical points at which justice institutions in the region have been affected. Focusing on shared *critical junctures* provides a common comparative narrative. It lays the foundation for a deeper understanding of modern judicial institutions and how they are shaped and are still embedded in personal-clientelist structures, with far-reaching consequences for courts and the rule of law in the region.

Throughout the region, precolonial state formation, colonial state-building, the postcolonial independence struggle and modernization, and the third wave of democratization at the end of the Cold War all provided impetus to the development of current justice institutions.

2.1 Precolonial Times: State Formation and Personalized Justice

Given the fluid national boundaries and transitory populations before the arrival of colonizers, local strongmen generally exercised judicial authority based on customs, religion, or local codes (or all three) or sometimes by administrative extensions of empires, kingdoms, and sultanates (Taylor 1999, 137–181; Day 2002). Except in Vietnam, which inherited the Chinese Imperial Code, religion was a defining factor. Buddhist legal traditions prevailed in much of continental Southeast Asia with support from royal decrees and customary village dispute settlement systems. Hinduism had a considerable influence across much of archipelagic Southeast Asia. From the early fifteenth century onwards, Islam began to be influential, especially in peninsular Malaya, Indonesia, and Mindanao. Nevertheless, Malay customary law (*adat*) remained by far the most typical, distinctive, and widespread form of customary law in the region (Harding 2015).

Thus, unlike in European states that came into existence based on warfare and taxation (Tilly 1975), the particularity of state formation in Southeast Asia meant that the application of law and the administration of justice were highly variable. No single power ever controlled all or even most of the region, nor did any leave a lasting and widespread legal impression (Hall 1981), although several empires and kingdoms, both mainland (e.g., Champa, Angkor, Pagan, Ayuttahya) and maritime (e.g., Srivijaya, Majapahit), came and went in Southeast Asia. Scholars tend to consider many of these early empires and kingdoms as loosely organized around a king whose person and ritual behavior constituted an "exemplary center" based on charisma and ritual "theatre"(Geertz 1980). Except for fourteen-century Vietnam, these kingdoms generally appear to have been dominated by "men of prowess," who appropriated Indian ideas about divine powers and kingship to create *mandalas*, sacred centers and spaces (Wolters 1999). Rather than being premodern "states," most of Southeast Asia was dotted with such centers – "a particular and often unstable situation in a vaguely definable geographical area without fixed boundaries ... where smaller centres tended to look in all directions for security" (Wolters 1999: 1717).

Nevertheless, there were some efforts to codify laws and administer justice systematically. For instance, when Malacca made Islam the state religion in the fifteenth century, Islamic law was integrated with Malay customary law. Thereafter, when the laws were codified in the late fifteenth and early sixteenth century, it became the Chief Minister's duty to apply the code in the name of the ruler (Lindsey and Steiner 2012). Similarly, Buddhist kingdoms on the mainland adopted Hindu *dharmasastras* (e.g., the Code of Manu) to various degrees and applied Buddhist teachings in royal courts. Siam's 1805 Law of the Three Seals was influenced by the Buddhist Dhammasat and was meant to guide officials and judges (Hooker 1978, 17–48). Similar efforts were also visible in the codes of the Le dynasty in Vietnam in the fifteenth to the eighteenth century (van Tai 1982).

In sum, judicial authority in precolonial times relied for the most part on customary and religious sources. It was traditionally tied to the sacral qualities of the ruler's person, regalia, and palaces. This meant that justice and other institutions were highly personalized, setting powerful path dependencies on which to build long-term patrimonial-institutional legacies.

2.2 The Colonial Period: Weberian Transplants and Bifurcated Justice

These dynamics changed in 1511 when the fall of Malacca to the Portuguese announced the arrival of the colonial powers (Table 2). Gradually, the colonizers changed the basis of political power and political legitimacy by replacing traditional sacred rule with secular bureaucratic principles. By the late nineteenth century, the legitimacy of colonial governors in Myanmar, Malaysia, and Indonesia was anchored on an efficient civil service and military establishment.

Table 2 Colonial period, Southeast Asia

	Colonial Power	Start of Colonization	Year of Independence	Legal System
Brunei	Britain	1888	1984	Common law
Cambodia	France	1863	1954	Civil law
Indonesia	Dutch	1619	1949	Civil law
Laos	France	1893	1954	Civil law
Malaysia	Britain	1786	1957	Common law
Myanmar	Britain	1826	1948	Common law
The Philippines	Spanish	1565	–	Mixed
	American	1898	1946	
Singapore	Britain	1819	1965	Common law
Thailand	–		–	Civil law
Timor-Leste	Portuguese (Indonesia)	1586 (1975)	1975 (2002)	Civil law
Vietnam	France	1859	1954	Civil law

Meanwhile, the Americans did away with Catholic-friar rule and expanded the reach of state institutions in the Philippines. The Dutch in Indonesia replaced the use of indigenous status symbols (e.g., *payung:* ceremonial sunshades) to come up with new secular ceremonies (Steinberg 1988). Even in Siam, the only country in the region that escaped direct colonization, King Chulalongkorn (1853–1910) continued the state and bureaucratic reforms of his father, King Rama IV (1804–68) toward a more comprehensive form of authority. This was done partly to support his state-building efforts as well as to prevent foreign encroachment (Pasuk and Baker 2014, 56, 66).

These developments had a direct effect on judicial authority. Initially, colonial governance logically meant that judicial authority was previously tied closely to the executive branch. As constitutional practice gained ground in the European capitals in the early nineteenth century, however, independent courts emerged almost universally as part of growing state administrations (Elson 1999, 150).

For instance, although judicial powers in the Philippines were vested in the governor-general in the early years of Spanish governance, they were shifted gradually to the *Real Audiencia* – a tribunal that began with both judicial and administrative functions but by 1861 had become a purely judicial body (Cunningham 1912). Similarly for Penang, Malacca, and Singapore, the First and Second Charters of Justice (1807, 1826) established the united Courts of Judicature to apply English common law and equity "as far as the local circumstances will admit" (Matson 1993, 762). In the Dutch Indies, reforms initiated under Governor Daendels (1807–10) came to full fruition in 1854 when the Colonial Constitution created a separate judicial branch, despite a dual segregated system of justice for indigenous Indonesians and Europeans (Juwana 2014, 315). Similarly during the French colonial expansion in Indochina, court structures were closely tied to the colonial administration before more differentiated structures were allowed to emerge (Thompson 1937; Brocheux and Hemery 2009). And in Siam, the traditional justice system was gradually modernized, culminating in the creation of a Ministry of Justice in 1891, followed by the first Western-style court procedures in 1901, and the civil law code in 1908 (Satayanurug and Nakornin 2014).

Although modern courts gradually came into existence, they had far less influence than the executive branch and were often part of a segregated system of justice. These reflected the different approaches of colonial powers to the application of law because of Southeast Asia's "plural societies" (Furnivall 1956 (1948)). For instance, the British introduced English law as the general law in the Straits Settlements, but its application was adapted somewhat for different groups, as was Islamic personal law. In the Dutch East Indies, the

Dutch initially adopted a policy of different "law populations," where each group would be subject to its own law (Lukito 2012). And while European laws had become the rule throughout Southeast Asia by the early twentieth century, the legal system was bifurcated in Malaysia, Indonesia, and Brunei, whereby ordinary courts apply common law and traditional religious courts applied *shari'a* law to Muslims in personal matters.

These exceptions aside, modern justice institutions and laws were closely tied to the colonial vision of the modern state as depersonalized, rational, and rule based. However, the bifurcated justice system ensured that the nascent judiciary dealt with only a small stratum of the population.

2.3 The Postcolonial Period: Modernist Ambitions and Neo-patrimonial Decay

Decolonization and nationalist struggles in the 1950s and 1960s were another impetus for state-building and, thus, justice system transformation. Nevertheless, how power was transferred within each colonial state proved important.

Where the colonial transition was gradual and negotiated, court structures were often left intact. In the former British colonies of Malaysia and Singapore (though not Myanmar), some colonial judges initially kept their positions and a right of final appeal to the British Privy Council was retained until the 1980s (Lee and Foo 2017; Tan 2017). Similarly, the Philippine courts transitioned gradually from US rule. The nationalization of the Supreme Court was achieved when the Commonwealth of the Philippines was created in 1935, but the US Supreme Court retained appellate functions until 1946. Thereafter, the Philippines and its public institutions became fully independent (Cruz and Cruz-Datu 2000).

In countries that underwent revolutionary nationalist struggles for independence, the changes were more drastic. The 1945 constitutional debates in Indonesia revealed widespread mistrust of the colonial courts. There were calls for an "integralist state" – one based on a more traditional and patriarchal rather than a rule-based Western-type system (Lev 1996). An integralist ideology that was hostile to individual rights, constitutional review, and clear separation of powers is widely seen as having initiated the eventual erosion of court autonomy and power (Elson 1999, 105–06). For similar reasons, after a tumultuous independence struggle, the constitutions of both North and South Vietnam gave the courts little autonomy (Nicholson 2007). In neighboring Cambodia and Laos, the initial situation was somewhat different because the traditional elites provided for institutional continuity after independence (Rose 1998).

However, many of the new Southeast Asian states had limited abilities to meet the high expectations of the independence struggle and the need for multiethnic societies to forge a single national identity. As a result, constitutional practice was eroded as authoritarian leaders arose from contentious and often violent internal politics that deeply influenced the construction of postcolonial states (Slater 2010). Not surprisingly, these developments also deeply threatened the independence of courts throughout the region.

In Indonesia, Sukarno's guided democracy period (1959–65) became the prelude to Suharto's authoritarian encroachment on court independence and professionalism under his New Order (1965–98). This eventually deprived the courts of public legitimacy (Bourchier 1999). Based on a "Burmese Way to Socialism" (1962–88), the military rule in Myanmar (1962–the present) eroded judicial independence and instrumentalized the courts (Cheesman 2011). The recurrent coups in Thailand (e.g., 1933, 1947, 1977, 1991) and recourse to executive emergency powers in the Philippines during martial law (1972–81) stifled the growth of justice institutions. Meanwhile, socialist rule in unified Vietnam (1976–present) and Laos (1975–present) severely constrained judicial autonomy and court functioning (Rose 1998; Nicholson 2007).

Far worse was the impact of the Khmer Rouge reign in Cambodia (1975–78), which demolished formal justice structures and physically eliminated the country's cadre of lawyers and judges (Donovan 1993; Kiernan 2008). Even in states like Singapore and Malaysia where post-independence developments were less dramatic, the close connection between the judicial and political elites and the emergence of single-party dominance of political structures – often with heavy reliance on patron–client relations – resulted in increased political constraints on the courts (Khoo 1999; Worthington 2001).

Thus, the general decline of constitutional practice in Southeast Asia and the rise of executive dominance severely impeded the development of the courts after decolonization. As a result, scholars perceived the judiciary not only as the weakest branch in the political system, but also as lacking resources, providing limited access to justice, and suffering from widespread corruption (Tate 1994). The decline of the courts corresponded with a gradual authoritarian turn in the region. This was exacerbated by a broad neo-patrimonial pattern of rule in which clientelistic political relationships, strong and unbound executives, and the use of public resources for political legitimation were combined. That pattern not only led to a fusion of public office and private interests but also undermined rule-based governance in the region.

2.4 The Third Wave of Democratization: The Persistence of Clientelism

At first glance, much has changed after the wave of democratization that swept through the region at the end of the Cold War. As political and economic liberalization has advanced in fits and starts, many countries in Southeast Asia have become more concerned not only about the rule of law but also about accountability and rights. The rule of law gained traction as new democracies emerged from authoritarian rule and consolidated democratic gains.

In the Philippines after the fall of Marcos, the 1987 constitution greatly expanded the powers of the Philippine Supreme Court. The constitutional drafters envisioned it as a critical bulwark against future authoritarian backsliding. Seizing on the weakness of the traditional elites after the Asian Financial Crisis, liberal drafters in Thailand (1997) and Indonesia (2001) used constitutional reform to insert new rights provisions and established specialized courts as guardians of constitutional rights (Klein 2003; Horowitz 2013). Meanwhile, the less than liberal regimes in Myanmar, Vietnam, and Cambodia chose constitutional and judicial reform as a way to tighten social control, enhance their legitimacy, and ensure credible policy outcomes (Ginsburg and Moustafa 2008).

Institutional changes have been critical to the expansion of judicial power since the 1980s. With political change roiling Asia in the 1990s, many Southeast Asian states revised their constitutions. Driven by liberal aspirations of a rule-based administrative and legal order (e.g., Thailand, Indonesia) or newly achieved statehood (e.g., Timor-Leste), the revisions have often empowered the courts through the expansion of judicial review and the establishment of institutional safeguards for the independence of judges. Moreover, they have often led to the creation of new constitutional, administrative, and other specialized courts with far-reaching powers in political areas such as elections and disputes related to electoral commissions, ombudsmen, and other oversight agencies. Anchored within the constitution, these new institutions are designed to be final and independent arbiters of administrative and constitutional conflicts rather than being dependent specialized courts ("chambers") within existing court structures, which have also been expanded since 2000 (Harding and Nicholson 2010; Chen and Harding 2018).

Supporting these developments has been a global discourse on good governance, which has considered the rule of law and the efficiency and independence of courts as instrumental to numerous desirable governance outcomes (Carothers 2003). In recent decades, bilateral and international agencies have dedicated considerable resources to judicial reform

(Armytage 2012). In general, they have been supporting reforms to improve court infrastructure and bolster judicial independence (World Bank 2003; Stephenson 2007). Typical reforms include changing procedures for the appointment of judges and security of tenure; creating judicial councils; setting up specialized courts, such as constitutional or commercial courts; updating criminal codes and modernizing the criminal justice system; subsidizing information management technology; and mandating transparency in trials and courthouses. Combined with the continuing professionalization of the legal sector through legal education and globalization of the profession, these institutional reforms have elevated judges vis-a-vis political actors, provided them more public visibility, and reinforced judicial self-governance. As a result, justice institutions and their power in the region are now very different from how they appeared just forty years ago.

Nevertheless, the results have been mixed at best. While the transformation of the judiciary in the region is undeniable and the expansion of the legal complex (e.g., lawyers, prosecutors, legal NGOs) has been equally impressive, they still suffer from a variety of political constraints. Authoritarian enclaves in Vietnam, Myanmar, Cambodia, and more recently Thailand have severely limited the independence of the courts. Equally important are shortcomings in democratic and semi-democratic settings, where executive encroachment on the courts is common primarily due to political clientelism, patronage, and patron–client relations still dominating political institutions in the region. Even in more competitive settings, oligarchic interests often exert disproportionate influence over political institutions (Winters 2012), and patterns of patronage have often been "massified" by democratization and devolution – greatly diminishing the performance of the institutions affected (Aspinall and Berenschot 2019).

The courts are not immune to such broad social dynamics. Except for Singapore and the socialist states of Laos and Vietnam, as Figure 1 indicates, Varieties of Democracy (V-Dem) data show that most states in Southeast Asia rank comparatively high (>0.5) for political clientelism, that is, the targeted contingent distribution of resources in exchange for political support (see Muno 2010). Neo-patrimonial rule is also pervasive in all but two countries (> 0.5), as indicated in Figure 2, wherein personalistic forms of authority pervade formal regime institutions, often along with clientelistic political relationships, unconstrained executives, and the use of public resources for political legitimation (see Erdmann and Engel 2006). In these settings, justice institutions are considered by scholars to be less independent, although the relationship is not always clear-cut, particularly where political clientelism in single party dominated settings is concerned. This might highlight that it is not just the degree of clientelism that matters, but also its characteristics as further explored in case study illustrations.

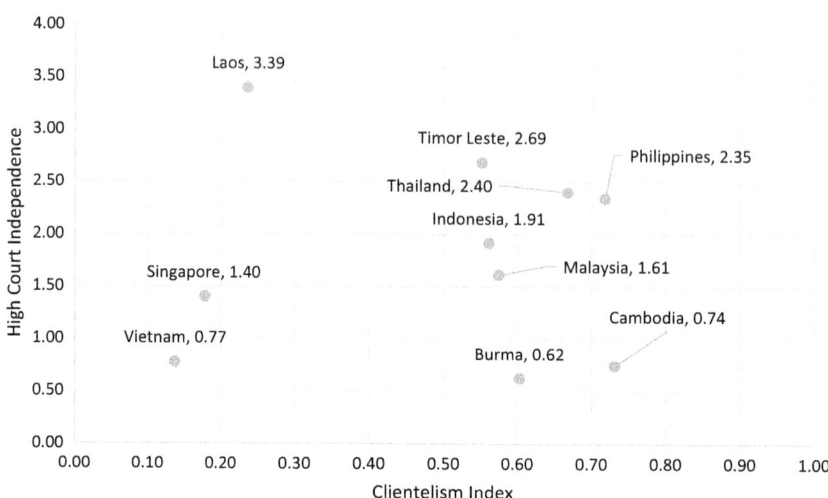

Figure 1 High Court Independence and V-Dem Clientelism Index, 1990–2020 averages

Source: V-Dem Dataset 2021.

Note: V-Dem's Clientelism Index is an aggregate index, comprising variables of vote buying (v2elvotbuy), particularistic or public good (v2dlencmps), and party linkages (v2psprlnks). The interval scale ranges from low (0) to high (1). High Court Independence is measured from low (1) to high (4).

In short, although the latest wave of democratization in the region brought considerable formal change, traditional politics in Southeast Asia remains rooted. As a result, a host of deep-seated and largely extralegal factors still severely limit the performance of courts in the region, among which are neo-patrimonial and clientelist dynamics. The continuing personalized nature of power and related clientelist and patronage-based structures lead to the courts suffering from the lack of a clear demarcation between public and private and formal and informal norms. This weakens institutional independence and forces us to rethink how judges behave through a broad relational lens marked by personal relationships, loyalties, and networks.

2.5 Southeast Asia's Courts at the Start of the Twenty-first Century: Independence under Threat?

The first two decades of the twenty-first century have proven to be a challenging environment for Southeast Asia's courts in light of democratic regression and growing executive backlash. Beginning with the military coup in Thailand in 2014, democracy appears to have receded across the region, in some cases abruptly as in Thailand or Myanmar while more gradually in the case of the

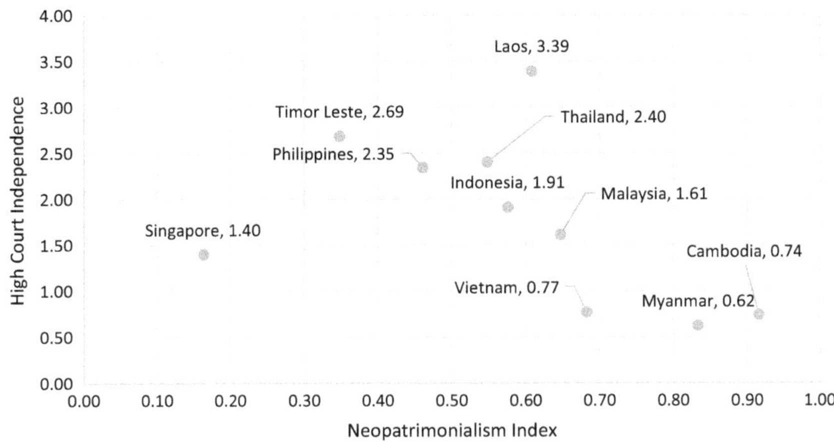

Figure 2 High Court Independence and Neo-patrimonial Rule Index, 1990–2020 averages

Source: V-Dem Dataset 2021.

Note: V-Dem's Neopatrimonialism Rule Index is an aggregate index, formed by taking the reversed point estimates (so that higher scores = more neopatrimonialism) from a Bayesian factor analysis model of the indicators for vote buying (v2elvotbuy), particularistic vs. public goods (v2dlencmps), party linkages (v2psprlnks), executive respects constitution (v2exrescon), executive oversight (v2lgotovst), legislature controls resources (v2lgfunds), legislature investigates the executive in practice (v2lginvstp), high court independence (V2juhcind), low court independence (v2jucnind), compliance with high court (v2juhccomp), compliance with judiciary (v2jucomp), electoral management body autonomy (v2elembaut), executive embezzlement and theft (v2exembez), executive bribes and corrupt exchanges (v2exbribe), legislative corruption (v2lgcrrpt), and judicial corruption (v2jucorrdc). The interval scale ranges from low (0) to high (1). High Court Independence is measured from low (1) to high (4).

Philippines, Indonesia, and Cambodia (Ockey 2023). Combined with authoritarian enclaves elsewhere (e.g., Vietnam, Laos), this has meant that all Southeast Asian countries are grouped in the bottom half of V-Dem's liberal democracy index. Except for Indonesia and Timor-Leste that are classified as electoral democracies, most countries are described as electoral or closed autocracies by 2022 (see Table 3).

Not surprisingly, such developments have directly affected the independence of the courts in the region. Except for Malaysia and Singapore, all other Southeast Asian countries show noticeable declines in the perception of high court independence over the last decade (Table 3). This democratic decline has occurred alongside the dissolution of courts (Thailand, Myanmar), removal of judges (Indonesia, the Philippines), and broader executive interference and intimidation of judges (Malaysia, Cambodia). Declining judicial independence

Table 3 Regime types and high court independence 2012 and 2022

Country	Regimes of the World (ROW) Classification (2022)	High Court Independence 2012 (range: 0–4, where higher numbers indicate greater court independence)	High Court Independence 2022 (range: 0–4, where higher numbers indicate greater court independence)
Brunei	N/A	N/A	N/A
Burma	Closed Autocracy	1	0.19
Cambodia	Electoral Autocracy	0.86	0.5
Indonesia	Electoral Democracy	2.71	2.42
Laos	Closed Autocracy	3.29	2.74
Malaysia	Electoral Autocracy	1.64	2.22
The Philippines	Electoral Autocracy	2.97	2.04
Singapore	Electoral Autocracy	1.31	1.62
Thailand	Closed Autocracy	3.37	1.67
Timor-Leste	Electoral Democracy	2.53	1.92
Vietnam	Closed Autocracy	1	0.44

Source: V-Dem Dataset, 2022.

has allowed governments increasingly to use government-aligned or controlled courts to silence and punish critics through the strict application of lèse-majesté, libel, or treason and espionage charges as shown in Thailand, Vietnam, and Cambodia (Section 4). A rare exception to this trend over the last decade has been Malaysia, where an increasingly fragmented political environment since 2008 appears to have allowed the Federal Court to regain a semblance of assertiveness and independence (Tew 2016).

The brief historical survey of courts in the region shows that an understanding of justice institutions must come to terms with how power has been traditionally organized and exercised, which helps explain the ongoing institutional fragility of courts. While products of colonial state-building efforts and despite their rapid professional transformation to modernity over the last century, courts are still deeply embedded in an institutional context of political clientelism, personalistic forms of authority, and political systems marked by the concentration of political power in the hands of small oligarchic elite groups. These factors deeply constrain the independence and performance of the courts, perhaps even more than the formal political regime itself.

There remain considerable differences between states in Southeast Asia in terms of the extent of political clientelism and neo-patrimonialism as well as the perceived independence of the high courts as shown in Figures 1 and 2. As expected, high levels of neo-patrimonial rule (>0.5) may correlate with low levels of court independence (e.g., Cambodia, Myanmar, Malaysia, Vietnam) and vice versa (e.g., the Philippines, East Timor). However, countries ranking low on the neo-patrimonial rule scale, like Singapore, also do poorly on court independence (Figure 2).

The relationship is even less clear for political clientelism (Figure 1). Malaysia, Myanmar, and Cambodia rank low on court independence and high on political clientelism as expected). However, Thailand, the Philippines, and Indonesia rank moderately high on the independence of their top courts despite high levels of political clientelism. Equally puzzling, Singapore and Vietnam rank low on high court independence, despite low levels of clientelism (Figure 1).

Such differences reveal that nuances exist within similar clientelist political settlements. The differences may depend on how power is organized – whether it is centered on a single dominant patron, as in authoritarian, sultanistic, or monarchical systems; or diffused into groups of competing political elites, as is common in competitive-oligarchic systems. As the discussion to come reveals, these differences shape the relational dynamics, including how political loyalties and networks influence engagement in high-profile "megapolitical" cases in the region, as discussed in Sections 3 and 4.

3 A Framework for Courts and Politics

The considerable diversity in histories, cultures, and legal and political systems in Southeast Asian countries poses considerable challenges to the comparative study of the courts and politics. In some countries (e.g., the Philippines, Indonesia, Thailand), high courts have forcefully asserted their powers and intervened in high-profile cases. In others (e.g., Singapore, Cambodia, Myanmar), high courts have been restrained, if not muted, when engaging in areas of politics. However, even where high courts appear to be "activist," local academic and legal actors have questioned judicial independence when judges appear to deviate from expected behavior or are accused of bending the law in favor of narrow political interests.

Given the diversity in the patterns of court behavior in the region, it is unsurprising that scholars have long debated factors that might drive variations in judicial engagement and have constructed typologies to conceptualize and map cases. For some scholars, this has meant explicitly linking a court's approach – whether limited, central, or risky – to the country's type of democratic regime, which could be dominant-party, dynamic, or fragile (Yap 2017). Other scholars have mapped the region's courts by their degree of "activism," linking them to the scope of their jurisdiction or the degree of public confidence and trust they have earned (Chen 2018, 27–8). There has also been a focus on the political–legal dynamics in each country, with Roux suggesting a typology of four ideal–typical "judicial regime types" – democratic and authoritarian legalism or instrumentalism – in which courts are situated based on the constraints exerted by law and politics (Roux 2018a, 2018b).

Highlighting differences in views of what might be driving the engagement of high courts in the region, such typological approaches are useful heuristics in capturing the ideal-type behavior of high courts and inviting broader conceptual and empirical work on the drivers of these observable institutional patterns and changes over time. Nevertheless, it is important to note that high courts are collegial courts that are made up of individual judges who bring their motivations and disagreements to the bench. These are illustrated in dissenting opinions and split decisions, particularly in contested high-profile cases, albeit less so in closed authoritarian settings. Ultimately, such patterns of judicial behavior raise questions about how judges make sense of their newfound powers and what explains judicial behavior in a context where it is acknowledged that both legal and nonlegal factors bear heavily on individual judges.

To capture both court and judge level dynamics, I start with a basic typology of high court behavior in Southeast Asia in areas of megapolitics – defined as cases that are of an inherently political nature and have the potential to divide a nation. While different from ordinary court jurisprudence, such cases are at the core of high court decision-making and often prove critical to public perceptions of judicial independence. This is followed by a reflection on how we may best understand the individual behavior of judges as part of a relational perspective on judicial behavior in Southeast Asia.

3.1 Mapping Judicial Politics in Southeast Asia

Academic engagement with the rise of courts in politics in Southeast Asia is closely tied to scholarship on the "judicialization of politics" in the region.

Nevertheless, there remains considerable debate about how to capture these developments systematically, considering the lack of agreement about how judicial engagement is conceptualized, what is driving it, and its effects. This is mainly because the concept of "judicialization" itself has been stretched to cover different, though sometimes interrelated, processes (see: Hirschl 2008b).

To illustrate, the abstract capture of social relations and popular culture by law as modern societies grow ever more complex – a process often described as "juridification" (see overview Blichner and Molander 2008) – deserves thoughtful separation from the much-analyzed expansion of the courts into public policy as part of "ordinary" constitutional rights jurisprudence. Another area of relevance is the even narrower reliance on courts and judges to deal with "megapolitics" – core political controversies and deep moral dilemmas related to purely political areas, such as executive branch prerogatives, electoral politics, and regime change (Hirschl 2008a, 99–100).

Narrowly, judicialization of politics refers to how judges, in exercising judicial review, influence public policy, as constitutional or supreme courts come to dominate policymaking that was previously the prerogative of legislatures and executives (Sieder, Schjolden, and Angell 2005a, 3). More broadly, judicialization encompasses not only the expansion of the scope of "judge-made law" but also the increased presence of judicial processes and court rulings in political and social life, such as when social actors use the courts to advance their interests, when political actors become more responsive to court actions, or when state legitimacy is increasingly constructed in terms of the rule of law (Domingo 2004, 108–10).

In both cases, judicialization is marked by more deference to the courts, as bureaucratic and political actors find themselves constrained by judicial review of administrative action or by political decision-making shaped by higher-order principles articulated by judges. As high courts are transformed into bodies making major political decisions, they gain more influence on aspects of governance than their traditional judicial role would allow.

However, a closer look reveals that the process of judicial repositioning and judicial self-assertiveness is hardly linear. Instead, as shown in Southeast Asia, it is marked by considerable diversity. Therefore, in regard to court engagement with megapolitics, it can be helpful to think in terms of a basic typology of ideal types of court behavior – judicial activism, judicial muteness, judicial restraint, and politicization of the judiciary – that reflect two dimensions that can be identified clearly from the literature: (a) de facto judicial independence (an aggregate of a court's structural independence, the extent to which judges are willing to intervene, and the support from political elites for independence); and (b) the extent to which judges are involved in areas of megapolitics.

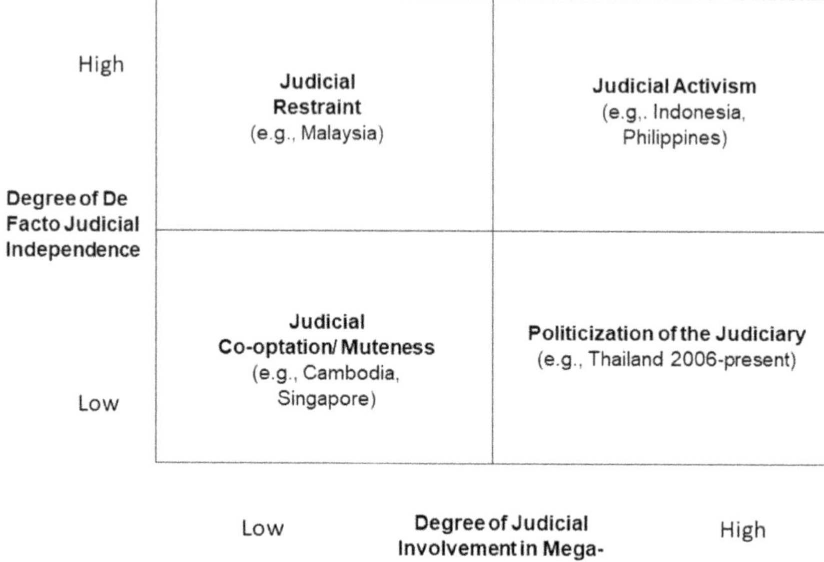

Figure 3 Patterns of judicial politics in Southeast Asia

Note: degree of de facto independence is measured by V-Dem High Court Independence variable five-year average, 2016–21 (scale 0–4; country values over 2 are considered "High," less than 2 as "Low"); degree of judicial involvement is drawn from a count of high court cases mentioned in the two leading newspapers and/or constitutional law journals over a five-year period (2015–2020) (count of more than 20 considered "high here")

Drawing on available data from 2015–20, we can then place representative examples from Southeast Asia on the matrix for given periods of time (Figure 3).

As illustrated here, it is conceptually possible to identify four different patterns of high court involvement in politics when taking into account these two dimensions, thus highlighting nuances of what the judicialization trend entails in the region:

• **Judicial activism** describes a situation in which high courts seize on their independence to become actively engaged (if not interventionist) in high-profile political cases when exercising judicial review. It will often involve courts going beyond the applicable law to consider broader societal implications, thus ignoring precedent and expanding jurisprudence into areas beyond their traditional purview, with far-reaching consequences for political governance and separation of powers.

• **Politicization of the judiciary** similarly captures a pattern of high court involvement in high-level political cases, albeit one where the high courts lack judicial independence and autonomy. This pattern is often linked to court stacking or undue influence over judges, in which the court acts as an extended arm of the government and/or as powerful actor in the political system, as illustrated by decisions favoring consistently one party to a conflict; questionable interpretations of the law, and gradual erosion of the legitimacy of the court to act as an independent arbiter in the eye of the public.

- **Judicial restraint** is a pattern whereby high courts, despite sufficient independence and autonomy to adjudicate cases of political relevance, often decide to do so in a highly restrictive manner and favor the status quo – for instance, when emphasizing that decisions should be consistent with previous jurisprudence (e.g., the principle of stare decisis); a conservative approach to who can apply (e.g., standing, grant of certiorari); and an often narrow, hyper-legalistic interpretation of constitutional questions and/or redirecting cases to other branches, when considering the issue of a case as political and not legal.

- **Judicial muteness** describes a similar situation of courts seeking to evade adjudication of high-profile cases, albeit in an environment where the courts often lack independence and internal autonomy. In settings where considerable pressure is exerted on judges and political actors are able to control the nature of political contestation, high courts have often fewer cases to decide. In the rare instance when confronted with a case, politically relevant cases are dismissed outright and deflected. This can be done through narrow legal interpretation or noting that actions by political branches have rendered the case moot. Hence, high courts play no meaningful role in the constitutional landscape and social actors largely dismiss courts as a legitimate outlet to arbitrate political conflict.

To be sure, these patterns of judicial politics are slightly overdrawn for illustrative purposes and not always easily distinguishable. The difference between judicial *restraint* and judicial *muteness* largely relates to whether the courts have the autonomy to choose on their own to withdraw from areas of megapolitics. Similarly, patterns of judicial activism might easily flip into a pattern of politicization when political elites exert control over the court in reaction to courts expanding their involvement in politics.

As the case study descriptions in Section 4 will demonstrate, the relationship among courts, law, and politics is highly fluid and the degree of judicial involvement can swing widely not only from country to country but also within a country over time. This vacillation may be due to exceptional events that propel judges into the political fray or possibly because political actors respond to court activism with institutional changes that curb the powers of judges. And in other situations, courts might decide to strategically avoid political confrontation by retreating to "formal-legalism" (i.e., a narrow formalist approach to the interpretation of the legal text), thus temporarily deviating from long-term patterns.

Notwithstanding such caveats, it is clear that the typology (Figure 3) provides a useful heuristic to provide rigor to the study of the courts, politics, and the judicialization trend in Southeast Asia. That institutional practices become ingrained not only allows us to capture distinct country patterns at a given point in time but also makes it possible to identify trajectories of judicial politics over time. As a result, the typology directs analytical attention to the conditions in which certain judicial patterns emerge and drivers change over time. It might also trigger debate about how these patterns shape modes of governance with respect to the rule of law, accountability, and the protection of rights.

3.2 Understanding Change, Evaluating Effects

What drives changes in judicial patterns? The comparative judicial politics literature highlights growing acknowledgment that explanations might not be based on a single factor but on a confluence of factors. Among these are enduring national, institutional, and political structures (e.g., political regime features, the political and legal powers of the courts, and international influences); contemporary political dynamics that press courts to take more responsibility for governance and public policy (e.g., intense support from current leaders, social and political movements); and the incentives, capacities, and motives of individual judges (Kapiszewski, Silverstein, and Kagan 2013a). Seeking to complement dominant approaches to judicial behavior, scholars have also drawn attention to historical and ideational factors – thus drawing attention to the institutional environment of the court itself and highlighting how institutions do not merely impose constraints on behavior but also become constitutive for preferences (Whittington 2000; Hilbink and Woods 2009).

The change in judicial patterns requires empirical attention to three distinct analytical levels that are in close interplay with each other:

- **Institutional factors:** captures formal powers of the court and regime features related to the separation of powers provided in the constitution and relevant legislation as well as informal norms within society and the court itself that constrain judicial behavior;
- **Societal Structures:** highlights the broader social embeddedness of the court and its judges within the country's professional–legal complex (e.g., breadth and depth of law association), elite structures (e.g., fractured or consolidated), and broader patterns of how power is formally and informally distributed and structured (e.g., degree and structure of clientelism);

- **Actors:** refers to judicial leadership (e.g., Chief Justice) as well as networks (e.g., ideational, material, personalistic) of high court judges, both on and off the bench, and their influence in shaping the behavior and motivations of judges and the court bench at large.

These factors come together in shaping patterns that high courts exhibit to various degrees. Changes in the power of the court as part of constitutional and judicial reforms often provide the basis for judicial leadership to steer courts to exhibit greater assertiveness when presented with the opportunity to do so. Likewise, when elites and/or the political landscape become fractured, political cases tend to emerge and throw the court into the political fray while also giving the courts more room to chart an independent path. And when courts face backlash, networks between the high court and the legal community can become critical in ensuring that courts maintain their independence and that court judgments are implemented and enforced. Hence, while highly contextual, analysis of these levels and their interplay allow a broader understanding of why judicial patterns change and/or might be stable over time.

Unsurprisingly, different views on the drivers of judicial patterns have led to different conclusions on how to evaluate the growing role of courts in politics. Scholars working to anchor judicialization within the macro processes of democratization and modernization (Shapiro 1999; Sunstein 2001) or the spread of rights consciousness and legal mobilization by civil society (Epp 1998; Slaughter 2000) have generally embraced the expansion of judicial review and court empowerment as a means to offer greater protection to citizens and to deepen democracy (Dworkin 1990; Ackerman 1997). On the other hand, authors of the structural school have been more cautious. Some authors see the growing role of the judiciary as conducive to deepening democratic governance by transforming political conflict into constitutional dialogue and providing a nonpartisan forum for grievances (Ginsburg 2014). Meanwhile, others have drawn attention to self-interested strategic actors and the role of elites in judicialization and have raised concerns that the process is anti-democratic and a move toward "juristocracy" (Hirschl 2004).

While the debate has often been empirically weak, if not outright normatively charged (Hilbink 2008), it highlights the inherent tension between judicial empowerment and areas of governance. It reminds us that judicial self-assertion is hardly a predictable process ——judicial actors are often deeply embedded in an illiberal past (Domingo 2004, 121). It further exposes the danger that as judicial systems become more salient, policymakers may also seek to influence the judiciary. It needs to be acknowledged that judges are strategic actors in their own right – pursuing goals ranging from protecting institutional interests and building engagement with the public to their own preference-driven policy goals (Kapiszewski 2011). Recognizing the agency of judges, then raises a relevant question: how do judges make decisions?

3.3 Rethinking Judicial Behavior of Judges in Southeast Asia

How to explain judicial behavior – what makes judges accept, deny, or decide cases as they do and what forces are likely to influence their decisions – has traditionally been at the center of the judicial politics scholarship. These questions emerged in response to traditional normative studies of how judges *ought* to decide cases and the formalist-legal view that judges decide purely by interpreting and applying the law (Friedman 2006; Leiter 2010). Instead, grounded in a tradition of legal realism (see Tamahana 2010), scholars have suggested numerous variables that enter into decision-making in high courts, whether Supreme or Constitutional. Personal attributes and attitudes matter (e.g., policy preferences, personal attitudes to outcomes, and policies). Interaction within the bench matters (e.g., natural pressure for consensus, concern for court reputation, or a common desire to empower the court over competing political and judicial forces). Psychological effects, biases, and party politics might come into play, such as in engendering loyalty to the appointer. Finally, these variables interact within a specific constitutional and doctrinal context, some with more, others with less legal formalism.

The theory used in the analysis affects the relative importance of these variables (good overview, Baum 2006; Posner 2008). The *legal* model assumes that judges decide in conformity with laws and precedents (Bailey and Maltzman 2011). It supports an image of judges as neutral and apolitical, using technical interpretation skills to ascertain the law that best applies to the specific case (Shapiro 1981). *Attitudinal* theorists argue, however, that ideological positions and policy preferences shape judicial decisions, especially in courts of last resort (Segal and Spaeth 1993, 2002). They downplay the influence of the letter of the law and portray judges as focused on legal policy (Baum 1994). The *strategic* model of judicial decision-making, also guided by the notion of judicial policy preferences, acknowledges that judges take into account the views of other actors and the institutional context – and may even deviate from a preferred outcome to take those views into account (Epstein and Knight 1998; Spiller and Gely 2010; Epstein and Weinshall 2021).

A full discussion of these theories is beyond the scope of this section. It is sufficient to say that while these models have proved useful, recent academic debates have increasingly raised concerns about how well certain models travel beyond the West (e.g., Dressel, Sanchez Urribarri, and Stroh 2018; Roux 2018b). There are good reasons for this limited applicability: legal, attitudinal, and strategic accounts all tend to assume that political institutions and legal systems are solidly institutionalized despite being hardly the case in the Global South. Some also portray judges as insulated conflict adjudicators motivated by individual preferences and engaging with other legal and political actors solely to advance their own goals.

Nevertheless, the motivations for judicial behavior are complex. In Southeast Asia, ideological divisions are often absent or trumped by primordial and clientelist affinities. Moreover, rapid changes in the legal environment have meant that legal constraints are still weak. Dominant informal practices generate greater uncertainty, and thus less rational expectations and incentives than current models would predict (Dressel, Sanchez Urribarri, and Stroh 2017). Combined with limited empirical support for current models of judicial behavior in the region, it is not surprising that attention has shifted more generally to the interplay between law and politics (Roux 2018b).

Even in Western settings, the singular focus on the legal policy preferences of judges has been criticized. Increasingly, studies have acknowledged that, being human, judges may pursue a host of goals beyond legal policy. These range from personal standing with the public and legal audiences (Baum 2006); career considerations and workload (Posner 2008); or maintaining collegial relations on the bench (Friedman 2006). Some of these authors view this as utility-maximizing strategic behavior. However, such focus on interactions also highlight how peers affect individual behavior, thus opening new avenues for studying psychological and relational effects. These relational effects may stem from on-bench group dynamics (e.g., Fischman 2013; Hazelton, Hinkle, and Nelson 2023) or from interactions of judges with others in the courtroom and beyond (Ginsburg and Garoupa 2015; Appleby and Lynch 2021). In fact, rather than assuming that the preferences of judges are fixed and exogenous, as most models do, the relational perspective sees the dynamics emanating from informal institutional relations as constitutive of how judges form preferences.

These debates have resonated strongly with studies of courts in the Global South, where scholars have long urged a move beyond formal "parchment" institutions to consider the role of informal institutions – defined as "rules and procedures that are created, communicated and enforced outside officially sanctioned channels" (Helmke and Levitsky 2004, 725). It is the interplay of both formal and informal institutions that matters to the performance of institutions, especially how informal institutions accommodate, complement, substitute for, or compete with formal institutions (Helmke and Levitsky 2006).

As a direct outgrowth of these institutional debates, sociolegal scholarship has opened a new line of inquiry about judicial politics that seeks to rethink the relationship-based behavior of judges. Drawing on anecdotal evidence on the influence of judge networks in Africa, Asia, and Latin America, this new scholarship has used a relational perspective to explain variations in outcomes such as judicial autonomy, ideational diffusion, patronage appointments, and even the actual decisions of judges (Staton 2010; Trochev and Ellett 2014; Ingram 2016b). Recognizing the importance of informality in less institutionalized settings – especially the critical role of informal relationships – this new scholarship has shifted to how judges participate in various circles of social interaction. It moves away from institutional constraints and the individual characteristics or attributes of a judge (the "node") to her or his relational contacts, connections ("ties"), and interaction with other individuals and collective actors (Box-Steffensmeier, Christenson, and Levitt 2016; Ingram 2016b).

Southeast Asia provides fertile ground for such a perspective. The region has often been analyzed in terms of how patrimonialism, clientelism, and personalized politics are expressed in political institutions (Jacobs 1971; Crouch 1986; Hutchcroft 1998). Although these approaches have rarely been applied to the courts, socio-anthropological accounts have regularly illuminated the different legal and judicial dynamics within the region, such as the importance of relationship-based legal exchanges and customary notions of justice within courts and law enforcement agencies. These dynamics are hardly captured by current formal–institutional rules (e.g., Engel 1978; Pompe 2005; McCargo 2020). Despite the appearance of modern practices, widely dispersed patterns of judicial clientelism and corruption, regular breaches and circumvention of professional ethics, and general public perceptions of political loyalties playing out on the high court bench suggest that the dynamics at play in the region differ considerably from what might be expected from theories of judicial behavior developed in the West.

The principal reason for the disparity is not that institutions are simply weak but rather that formal and informal practices are closely intertwined in non-Western polities and personal interactions heavily affect how institutions, such as courts, operate. Scholars have argued that politics in many developing countries is characterized by "formal political rules and institutions [that] are shadowed by a netherworld of personalized political relationships and networks, secretive deal-making, trading of favors, corruption, and a host of informal and shadowy practices" (Aspinall and Berenschot 2019, 11). While broadly describing political practices applicable to the region, this informal–relational landscape can also affect the agency of judges and other actors in the legal system, with serious consequences for how courts operate and how judges make decisions.

Hence, executive interference and co-optation, judicial clientelism, and sophisticated networks of judicial corruption all influence how courts in the region operate. Informal institutions are deeply rooted and often replace, or compete with, formal rules to constitute the real rules that shape the work of judges. Within the personalized institutional context, informal relationships and wider networks are critical constraints and occasional enablers that affect a variety of areas of judicial autonomy, independence, and decision-making.

Three questions appear critical in analyzing this relational focus:

- Which types of relationships and networks matter for judges in their institutional context?
- What informs the ties between judges and other social actors and how are they maintained?
- How do informal relational dynamics affect the behavior of judges? How do they affect related areas, such as appointments, court reform, and decision-making?

The following discussion may offer some answers to these questions through the lens of judge networks.

3.3.1 Formation and Maintenance of a Judge's Network

There are innumerable types of networks, defined here as groups or systems of social interactions and personal relationships adapted to social circumstances (Scott 2013). Both anecdotal and empirical evidence suggest that the types of networks most relevant to a judge are those based on friendship; recruitment to the bench; political interests, whether partisan or ideological; patronage and clientelism; and those based on cultural, regional, or religious ties. Such networks generally form through shared pathways and characteristics and repetitive interaction (e.g., socialization in law school, shared years on the same court, or membership in legal associations). There are differences in the extent to which they are formally recognized (e.g., judges' associations, university alumni associations, and legal fraternities and sororities) or are mainly informal (e.g., friendships). Likewise, a judge's networks may differ in whether it yields horizontal (peer relations) or vertical (clientelist) ties and may vary in the strength of their ties. In short, depending on the setting and intent, relationship dynamics are guided by various degrees of informality, the extent to which they operate openly or shrouded in secrecy, and their strengths and directionality.

From a judge's perspective, there are perhaps three spatial–relational dimensions that may apply. There are *on-bench* relationships and networks that include the daily interactions with colleagues a judge is involved with socially and professionally. This is most notable when deciding cases in a panel or *en banc*. By extension, there are also the relationships a judge has built with colleagues across courts, including friendships and professional networks a judge brings to the bench from previous assignments in lower or specialized courts or as part of a professional circle of peers. Finally, there are *off-bench* social relationships and network circles that involve members of the legal community and political and private actors that the judge interacts with inside and outside the courtroom. These could stem from their personal life, through the career and appointment process, or as part of clientelist and corrupt networks where decisions are exchanged for material benefits.

The motivations of judges to establish and sustain social ties might differ. Some networks are based on material exchanges, while others on ideational and nonmaterial interests. The material exchange of money for decisions or trading clientelistic benefits (e.g., judicial appointments or contracts related to court operations) might describe one end of the continuum and ideational communities formed around shared goals and beliefs, the other. As a result, some ties might be short-lived because they are geared to a transactional goal (e.g., career promotion), while others may have been nurtured for years as part of regular clientelist exchanges (e.g., exchange of votes). Meanwhile, some ideational networks can be characterized in terms of long-term personal bonds based on university and school affiliations, friendships, or regional and ethnic loyalties that may date back decades before a justice ascends to the highest bench. The type, intensity, and length of these relations might matter when evaluating the strength of these ties and the informal pressures that might compromise the impartiality of a judge.

The ties between actors in these networks are based on a "bundle of relational expectations" (Fuhse 2015, 36). They can be characterized by different interpersonal dynamics or combinations thereof, such as reciprocity, self-presentation, individual benefit, ideational affinities, or authority and loyalty. It might be expected that a friendship network will be dominated by self-presentation or emotive and ideational affinities. On the other hand, career development networks might be motivated by reciprocity or individual benefits. Meanwhile, networks based on patronage, clientelism, or brokerage might be characterized mainly by transactional dynamics, underpinned by authority, loyalty, or shared regional, cultural, or kinship ties. Network theory suggests that the more the ties overlap and appear multistranded between individuals or groups, the ties will not only be more intense but also result in a stronger network (Mitchell 1974, 283). Nevertheless, infrequent, single-stranded, or tenuous ties may also have an effect (Granovetter 1973).

Thus, different types of networks affect how judges behave (see Table 4) based on a variety of different relational ties in a variety of areas, such as when judges

Table 4 Influence of networks on judges

Type of Network	Characteristics of Relational Ties	Possible Outcomes in Terms of Judicial Behavior
Professional	Goal-oriented; career advancement	Judicial appointments
Friendship-based	Shared experiences; self-presentation; reciprocal; emotive	Judicial decision-making; case management
Ideational	Shared ideas; reciprocity	On-bench factional voting; internal reform dynamics
Political	Ideological; partisan	On-bench voting; on-bench pursuit of policy preferences
Sociocultural	Primordial loyalties based on regional, religious, or cultural traits	On-bench voting; nepotism in appointments; court legitimacy
Patronage/clientelism	Exchange-focused, dyadic, contingent, asymmetric, iterated, hierarchical	Delivery of judicial decisions in exchange for rewards; case management; appointments

decide to protect the independence of the courts or influence decisions within a collegial court. In terms of internal organization and performance, they may also affect how careers progress on and off the bench and even after retirement.

A few qualifiers are in order: The table should not be considered comprehensive. It merely provides an outline to capture the relational dimension emerging in the judicial politics literature. It should also be clear that judges are often part of several overlapping networks and might move in and out of networks over time or due to personal circumstances. Some networks might gradually evolve: gender groupings might start as friendships before solidifying as professional networks. Networks might also not be equally inclusive or tight. Some are close-knit while others are more loose-knit and they may affect judge's behavior in varying degrees. Viewed as a particular form of social capital that individuals can employ to enhance their advantages and opportunities, peer, friendship, or kinship networks based on similarities (e.g., bonding capital) may bind more forcefully than outward-looking professional or political ties (e.g., bridging capital). However, their relevance to judicial behavior will depend greatly on the circumstances, including the pressure exerted on a given judge by a broad judicial network.

3.3.2 Effects of Judicial Networks

Journalistic and academic literature suggest areas where networks have influenced what judges do. For instance, networks of judges and political actors have been found to play out forcefully in the composition of the bench, particularly when the executive is making final decisions about appointments (Scribner 2004; Malleson and Russell 2006). Even where judicial commissions are charged with preparing shortlists or there is an established multitrack appointment process, networks actively seek to influence selections (Chua et al. 2012). Friendships or ideational affinities might also influence the decisions judges make in court, help diffuse ideas, or create reform coalitions within the courts (Ingram 2016b). Patronage relationships and corrupt networks may affect the assignments of judges and deference in decisions to other branches of government (Basabe-Serrano 2015). These patronage relationships may continue to exert influence after high court justices retire and are rewarded with government appointments (Gomez 2009). International networks of clerks and judges may be critical to the diffusion of ideas within the court system. Finally, alliances between judges and societal actors are often critical to determining how much autonomy judges actually have (Trochev and Ellett 2014).

Illustrations of how networks shape judicial behavior can be found in the areas of appointments and decision-making, and the legitimacy of the courts in Southeast Asia.

Networks and Appointments

In Southeast Asia, judicial appointments have traditionally been the focal point of formal and informal network activities. This is particularly true for appointments to the highest court for good reason: appointment opportunities to the highest bench are few and potentially far-reaching, and the responsibility to appoint high court judges often falls to a single appointer, such as the executive. As a result, networks may try to influence the selection of their preferred candidate even when independent appointment commissions have been tasked to vet the candidates and prepare a shortlist.

This is not to say that institutional rules do not matter. There is a great variety of appointment arrangements in the region with countries anchoring judicial appointments to their Constitutional or Supreme Court in the executive (e.g., the Philippines), legislature (e.g., Thailand), or a multitrack process (e.g., Indonesia). In line with international best practices (e.g., Cape Town Principles on the Roles of Independent Commissions in the Selection and Appointments of Judges, 2016), some countries have established independent, professional appointment commissions to assist in the vetting and shortlisting of candidates (Lee and Pittard 2017b).

Nevertheless, practices from the region show the limits of these institutional processes given the widespread activities of informal judicial networks. For instance, although the legal community widely perceived the establishment of Malaysia's Judicial Appointments Commission in 2003 as positive, the Commission has failed to stop the government from exerting pressure on judges in politically sensitive cases or influencing the appointment of judges considered loyal in politically sensitive cases, propelled by historical single-party dominance and political influence over promotions in the public service (Thomas 2021).

Similarly, the Judicial and Bar Council (JBC) in the Philippines was established in 1986 after the overthrow of President Marcos to insulate appointments to the courts from the wide perception that judges were beholden to the executive and politicians. Nevertheless, it has suffered from informal lobbying attempts of brokers to interfere in its shortlist. One factor may be that the pool of candidates is still very shallow (Gatmaytan and Magno 2011). This is exacerbated by the magnified influence of the executive branch in the hyper-presidential system (Rose-Ackerman, Desierto, and Volosin 2011).

Perhaps because of dangers like these, Indonesia has opted for a multitrack appointment system in which parliament, the president, and the Supreme Court each appoint a third of the justices to the Constitutional Court. This system is regarded as having ensured a good selection of regionally and professionally diverse candidates in the first decade of the court. Nevertheless, corruption scandals involving the court's justices have drawn attention to an increasingly politicized appointment process, particularly in parliament, where candidate horse-trading is widespread and candidates often actively rely on their political networks to lobby members of parliament to enhance their chances of nomination (Dressel and Inoue 2018b). Likewise, President Jokowi's (2014–24) growing executive influence vis-à-vis parliament during his second term over parliament, has meant a more disproportionate influence of the executive over judicial appointments.

While not unique to the region, what is clear from these developments is that politicized appointments to the high courts are an ever-present danger throughout Southeast Asia. In some ways, these dynamics appear more visible in authoritarian and socialist regimes in the region. Neither the Constitutional

Tribunal in Cambodia nor the Constitutional Council in Myanmar has ever been fully independent due to far-reaching political control and interference. Through the years, both benches have been altered and dissolved. Established in 1997 by the "People's Constitution," the Constitutional Court in Thailand has seen its bench suspended and then gradually altered by military-imposed constitutions, thus gradually tilting its membership toward royal-bureaucratic actors (Dressel and Tonsakulrungruang 2019).

Nevertheless, the role of informal networks in judicial appointments and career advancement is not always purely negative. Ideational and professional networks within and outside a court system provide important checks and balances. They can support institutional reform efforts or meritocratic selection practices. This is particularly so when the legal complex is well-organized and actively promotes accountability, which has happened in Malaysia and the Philippines (Halliday, Karpik, and Feeley 2014). Where they exist, judicial training academies provide opportunities, particularly among high court judges, to build professional networks via international conferences and training and exchange of personnel. In doing so, the academies can help reinforce integrity-based practices (De Visser 2016).

This process of professionalization is accelerated by the formation of regional working groups on emerging legal subjects, such as environmental law. These groups may be supported by international organizations and international foundations that promote the rule of law, such as the Asian Development Bank, the Asia Foundation, and the Konrad Adenauer Foundation. However, throughout Southeast Asia, the impact of these initiatives has been uneven as professional-legal networks have to contend with informal relational political constraints that undermine their reach and work (Armytage 2011, 2012).

Networks and Court Decisions

As a direct extension of influences on the appointment of judges, relational dynamics, and social networks also play out in court decisions, often as part of a judge's network (Box-Steffensmeier, Christenson, and Levitt 2016; Ingram 2016b). Drawing on growing empirical literature that has shown how neighbor or peers affect individual behavior in a variety of settings (e.g., educational achievements, criminal activity, investment decisions), judicial scholars have been drawing attention to how social interactions between judges on the bench might influence how they vote. This influence might be caused by endogenous effects (how individual behavior is influenced by the behavior of the group, such as when considering the effect of a dissent), or by contextual effects (how an individual's behavior is influenced by a factor characteristic of group members, such as when seniority or gender influences decisions) (Fischman 2015).

There is growing recognition that, in the courtroom, judges interact with lawyers and court personnel. In-court dynamics might influence the decisions of individual judges due to the psychological effects of self-presentation or reputation established between judges and their audiences (Baum 2010; Ginsburg and Garoupa 2015). Decisions might respond to the ideational influence of professional peer-to-peer networks of judges and court staff designed to share experiences, information, and standards of legal interpretation within the country and the region (Harlow and Rawlings 2007; De Visser 2016). However, others have also drawn attention to subtle informal influences of political and private actors that affect judges' decision-making (Llanos et al. 2014), or have described how judges embedded in corrupt and clientelist judicial networks have exchanged favorable judgments for material benefits (Basabe-Serrano 2015).

While the empirical exploration of relational and network-based effects on judicial decision-making in Southeast Asia is still in its infancy, how relational–judicial dynamics play out has been illustrated in academic, journalistic, and personal accounts from the region. Empirical studies of the Philippines Supreme Court have shown how appointees to courts are more likely to vote for the president who appointed them in high-profile cases (Escresa and Garoupa 2012). They have also shown how shared educational and professional ties among the members of the bench might accentuate this trend by providing incentives for cohort voting (Dressel and Inoue 2018a). Meanwhile, occasional scandals and whistleblower accounts allow for insights into some of the deeper dynamics of a judge's network. For instance, the former Chief Justice of the Constitutional Court in Indonesia was arrested for corruption related to a court decisions on an electoral matter involving a former party mate (Butt 2019a, 187). In Malaysia, several "poison pen" letters and whistleblower accounts by judges have provided insights into collusion and assignments of politically sensitive cases – such as the Anwar Ibrahim trials – to selected justices to foster desirable outcomes in exchange for career and material benefits (Trowell 2015). In Thailand, the military appointed Senate has enabled political networks to control the appointment of Constitutional Court judges, skewing the court's performance and professionalism in politically charged cases (Mérieau 2016; Tonsakulrungruang 2017).

While many of these dynamics take place in the shadowy world of informal practices, authoritarian regimes have often spent little time hiding them. Party membership of judges in socialist countries is common. In Cambodia, the courts are staffed by high-ranking members of and advisors to the Cambodian People's Party, which severely erodes the independence of the courts in political cases (West 2019). In many authoritarian settings, judges may be actively drawn into networks supporting the regime when hearing sedition and defamation lawsuits against opposition members, while at the same time limiting the role of defense lawyers or coordinating with other government agencies to restrict and criminalize political participation and expression (Streckfuss 2011; Yap 2017). It is not uncommon for observers to classify members of a high court bench as increasingly divided between "technical" and "political" judges, often directly reflecting the influence of internal and external judicial networks, even in settings such as Singapore (Worthington 2001, 516). Meanwhile, threats and the incidence of physical harm to judges and lawyers by state actors and plaintiffs are still credible means of enforcing required behavior when more subtle efforts to pressure a judge fail, as illustrated in Cambodia, Myanmar, and to some extent even in the Philippines (Amnesty International 2021).

Networks, Court Performance, and the Legitimacy of the Courts

Finally, the varied roles of judges' networks are also visible in areas of court performance and, by extension, in perceptions of court legitimacy. Poor performance of the courts concerning their administration, case management, and access to justice, is a perennial issue across Southeast Asia. Informal networks are widely acknowledged to matter greatly in these dynamics – both positive and negative.

Reports of how networks within and outside the courts have undermined the justice sector through corrupt activities and resistance to reform are common, particularly in post-authoritarian settings (Domingo and Sieder 2001; Hammergren 2007; Sieder 2010). Scholars have drawn attention to the dynamics within the judiciary, highlighting the often ambiguous stance of judges about judicial reform and new institutional structures (Domingo 2004). Studies have identified factors that motivate judges to take a stand for or against institutional reform – a choice often shaped by personal relations and ideational judicial networks (Ingram 2016a). Based on established scholarship on rights-oriented expansion and contraction of the judicial agenda elsewhere (Epp 1998; Hilbink and Woods 2009), studies have looked closely at how ideational networks animate and sustain judicial and legal change, including when progressive and conservative groups of judges are actively at odds or whether overseas training of judges influence how they behave (Hilbink 2007; Ingram 2016b).

These network dynamics can be illustrated in the uneven track record of judicial reform in Southeast Asia (Armytage 2012). Resistance of judges to the new Constitutional Courts in Indonesia and Thailand has been well-documented (Klein 2003; Pompe 2005). Nevertheless, court leaders (e.g., the Chief Justice) may succeed in mustering support for reform by building internal alliances, including with bar associations and international and bilateral partners and other civil society groups that can provide technical and financial support for reform. For instance, the visionary first Chief Justice of Indonesia's Constitutional Court, Jimly Assidique (2003–08), has often been credited not only with establishing the court itself but also with establishing esprit de corps and public legitimacy in its first decade (Hendrianto 2018). By contrast, ambitious reform efforts under different Chief Justices of the Supreme Court of the Philippines showed uneven success due to changes in leadership and justices' personal ability to rally support around their initiatives from their network (Vitug 2010, 2012).

Reform initiatives often reflect frustrations with the functioning and the legitimacy of the justice system that range from poor performance (long delays, corruption) to concerns over partisan appointments (court stacking). The lack of legitimacy, particularly of the high courts, is a particular issue in Southeast Asia's politicized environment, where the public has seen in varying degrees how judicial appointees might belong to political party networks (Vietnam, Cambodia); royal-monarchical networks (Thailand); ideological networks that reflect the dominant regime coalition (Malaysia); or the extended personal and political networks of presidents (the Philippines).

Combined with the careful public reading of regional, ethnic, and religious affiliations of judicial candidates common to many multiethnic states in the region, the mere perception of judicial networks that are unrepresentative can modify public opinion about the legitimacy of the courts. A case in point is Malaysia, where the public has regularly debated the ethnic and religious balance within the High Court, especially in the last decade as the Federal Court has become less diverse (Dressel and Inoue 2022). Observers have noted the disproportionate regional representation of the judges on the Constitutional Court in Indonesia, perhaps owing to the larger influence of regional judicial and political networks in lending support to these candidates (Dressel and Inoue 2018b, 169). Less noted, although possibly more pronounced, is the underrepresentation of women on the highest courts in the region even though women often outnumber male judges at the lower levels. Factors that might explain gender imbalance include institutional biases in the appointment process (e.g., male-dominated selection committees and appointer); limits on the candidate pool based on qualifications; self-selection, and "old-boys networks" (Crouch 2021).

An active civil society and moments of political transition can increase the prospects for alternative networks to gain ground. When Richard Malanjum was appointed as Chief Justice of the Federal Court of Malaysia (2018–19), as part of a postelection political transition, he was already a recognized dissenter in high-profile cases and became the first non-Muslim CJ in Malaysia. This appointment set a new tone for diverse views and minority representation on the bench. In the Philippines, female justices have relied on formal (i.e., the Philippine Women Judges Association) and informal networks to advance their causes. This may explain why there are more women on high courts in the Philippines than in regional peers. Judges also find themselves embedded in new professional networks that have formed around emerging issues, such as environmental law or gender-related violence with growing support from bilateral and multinational agencies. These professional networks can become the nuclei for addressing shortcomings in the justice sector that push for reform and advance professionalization. However, their ability to challenge deeply ingrained, corrupt networks can be tenuous, as illustrated by the "judicial mafia" in Indonesian courts that actively competes with professional networks (Butt and Lindsey 2010).

In sum, relational dynamics, and by extension networks, play a persistent role in influencing the work of courts and judges in Southeast Asia across various areas of judicial governance and behavior. Despite institutional norms to protect the independence of judges, judicial networks are able to penetrate the judiciary and influence the work of justices. In the hybrid-institutional context of the region, it is critical to evaluate the political regime and how power is organized.

The relational dynamics differ depending on whether the regime is centered on a single dominant patron, as in authoritarian, sultanistic, or monarchical systems; or diffused into groups of competing political elites, as is common in competitive-oligarchic systems. Where power is organized as a pyramid around a single patron, control is often easier to establish and judicial networks are more clearly aligned. By contrast, where there is more competition between power centers, fragmentation on the bench is also more likely. Institutional mechanisms, such as multitrack appointments or election of a Chief Justice from among peers on the bench may provide limited protection from the dynamics described, although such institutional safeguards are difficult to sustain in an environment where political and judicial elites regularly mingle both socially and professionally.

That is why, rather than focusing on the regime type alone (e.g., democratic, semi-authoritarian, authoritarian), it might be helpful to think in terms of different clientelist regime dynamics (e.g., patronal, hegemonic, competitive) with each shaping different court practices. Different clientelist regimes breed different network dynamics that influence judicial behavior and performance. The more dominant and hierarchical the clientelist structure is, the less room there is for competing networks. While authoritarian settings might be more clearly structured around a central patron, networks based on different ties (e.g., ethnic, regional, political, familial) might be able to compete for influence even in these settings. This pattern will be further illustrated in the country case studies in the next section

4 Case Studies from Southeast Asia

Exploring the diverse trajectories of courts and politics in Southeast Asia by applying the typology (Figure 3), this section will look at the behavior of Supreme or Constitutional Courts in the region, given that they are the courts most likely to be involved in megapolitics. Variation in clientelist regimes allows different network dynamics to exist within each political system.

For instance, in factionalized clientelist settings, such as a competitive oligarchic system like the Philippines, competing networks will extend to the judiciary. This is often mirrored by a factionalized Supreme Court bench. Similarly, Indonesia shows how institutional design can insulate the Constitutional Court, fostering a degree of activism. Nevertheless, networks will seek to exert influence on the judiciary in varying degrees. By contrast, in a patronal-clientelist regime like Thailand, where the monarchy dominates the clientelist structure, competing networks are stifled. This results in a judiciary that is easily politicized to favor monarchy-aligned actors, which also provides some insulation from competing interests.

In hegemonic-clientelist settings, the degree of cohesion amongst power-holders matters. More fragile hegemonic settings like Malaysia allowed the emergence of an independent Malaysian Bar. The Malaysian Bar has maintained strong links with the judiciary; in times of executive encroachment, the legal complex has provided support to the judiciary, while also holding it accountable to legal standards and practices despite political pressures. This has resulted in legalistic decisions broadly in line with judicial restraint. Finally, in strong hegemonic settings like Singapore, counter-hegemonic networks have been more contained. This has meant few linkages between judges and the legal complex, resulting in limited cases of political relevance reaching the high court. Hence, unlike in Malaysia, Singapore's regime has produced a deferential, if not muted behavior of the high court in high-profile cases.

The following case studies illustrate how relational–institutional dynamics linked to judicial networks and wider clientelist politics support and alter these judicial patterns.

4.1 Judicial Activism: Indonesia and the Philippines

The Indonesian Constitutional Court and the Philippine Supreme Court illustrate the existence of judicial activism. Both courts are closely tied to democratic transitions. The Indonesian Constitutional Court was established in 2003 as part of sweeping post-Suharto constitutional amendments. Since its inception, it has decided over 80 high-profile cases, 75 percent of which were decided against the government, often with a high dissent rate (Dressel and Inoue 2018b). The Philippine Supreme Court saw its powers reinforced by the 1987 post-Marcos constitution. From 1987–2020, it ruled on 70 megapolitical cases with 31 percent decided against the government and a consistently high dissent rate of 50 percent across administrations (Dressel, Inoue, and Bonoan 2023) These numbers highlight both the willingness of the courts to rule on high-profile cases, and also the work of civil society networks that petition courts to be involved in addressing political questions. Hence, it is clear that both courts have gradually moved from quiescence to become active and politically influential institutions in the post-authoritarian period (Mietzner 2010; Ciencia Jr. 2012)

The development of the Indonesian Constitutional Court is particularly telling (see overview: Butt 2015). In less than a decade, the court has confidently resisted parliamentary attempts to limit the exercise of its jurisdiction,[1] invalidated national legislation as unconstitutional,[2] and imposed obligations on the state based on principles implied in the constitution such as the protection of citizens from corruption and the right to a fair trial, access to justice, and legal aid.[3] The Constitutional Court has also become involved in economic questions, such as privatization,[4] public policy, such as in the allocation of the national education budget,[5] and contentious religious matters such as polygamy and blasphemy. Thereby, the Court has defined the place of Islam in Indonesia in the policy process.[6]

It is in electoral matters, however, that the court has seemed particularly activist, by engaging in cases with wider societal impact. It has not only decided several electoral disputes (Mietzner 2010, 407), but it also controversially allowed former members of the Communist Party (PKI, *Partai Komunis Indonesia*) to stand for the legislature on the grounds that the constitution protects citizens from discrimination.[7] Surprisingly, it also found the allocation

---

[1] MK Decisions: 004/PUU-I/2003; 013/ PUU-I/2003; 066/PUU-II/2004.

[2] MK decisions: 6/PUU-V/2007 and 012–022/PUU-IV/2006; 013/2003; 9/PUU-VII/2009 and 98/ PUU-VII/2009; 011–017/2003.

[3] MK Decisions: 006/PUU-I/2003; 006/PUU-II/2004.

[4] MK Decision 001–021-022/PUU-I/2003.

[5] MK Decisions 011/PUU-III/2005 and 026/PUU-III/2005.   [6] MK Decision 12/PUU-V/2007.

[7] MK Decisions 14–17/PUU-V/2007 and 15/PUU-VI/2008.

of parliamentary seats according to party rankings as unconstitutional, thus clearing the way for a fully open party system.[8] In an emergency decision two days before the 2009 presidential ballot, it further ruled that every eligible Indonesian with a valid identity card could vote.[9] Shortly thereafter, the Constitutional Court overturned a verdict of the Supreme Court, thereby siding with an election commission ruling that had questioned the parliamentary seat allocation that favored large parties.[10] Since then, the Constitutional Court has continued this activist stance, most notably in adjudicating electoral disputes in the contested presidential and legislative (2014, 2019) as well as local elections (Dressel and Inoue 2018b; Butt 2019b).

With a long history at the apex of the ordinary court hierarchy, the Supreme Court of the Philippines has been similarly activist. After the post-Marcos 1987 constitution expanded the scope of judicial review, the court quickly turned activist. During the Aquino presidency (1987–92), it invalidated presidential appointments,[11] restricted the sale of state property,[12] and invalidated the first oil deregulation law.[13] Subsequently, under President Ramos (1992–98), the Supreme Court rejected efforts to amend the constitution via the Initiative Referendum Act.[14]

In 2001, however, the court assumed a bold new political role after massive protests following the halted Estrada impeachment. In a controversial decision, the Court cleared the political deadlock by ruling on the resignation of former President Estrada and recognizing Vice-President Macapagal Arroyo as the new president.[15] Under the Arroyo presidency (2001–10), it invalidated a series of multi-billion-dollar contracts;[16] extensively reviewed violations of political and civil liberties cases;[17] rejected renewed efforts for constitutional change;[18] and struck down an agreement on ancestral domain between the Philippine government and the Moro Islamic Liberation Front.[19]

In both Indonesia and the Philippines, concerns grew that greater court activism might carry the ever-present danger of attempts by elites to politicize the court. In 2018, Chief Justice Sereno, who had been a staunch critic of President Duterte (2016–22), was unexpectedly removed by a majority vote of her peers in the Supreme Court via the questionable *quo-warranto* procedure.

---

[8] MK Decision 110–111-112–113/PUU-VII/2009. [9] MK Decision 102/PUU-VII/2009.

[10] MK Decision 110–111-112–113/PUU-VII/2009. [11] Brillantes v. Yorac, G.R. No. 93867.

[12] Garcia v. Board of Investments, G.R. No. 88637.

[13] Tatad v. Secretary of Energy, G.R. No. 124360. [14] Santiago v. Comelec, G.R. No. 127325.

[15] Estrada v. Arroyo, G.R. No. 146738.

[16] Agan Jr. v. Philippine International Air Terminals Co., Inc., G.R. No. 155001.

[17] BAYAN v. Ermita, G.R. No. 169838; Senate v. Ermita, G.R. No. 169777; David v. Arroyo, G.R. No. 171396.

[18] Lambino v. Comelec, G.R. No. 174153.

[19] Province of North Cotabato v. Government of the Republic of the Philippines, G.R. No. 183591.

This opened the floodgates for attempts by Duterte loyalists to remove other members of the bench who had been critical. The issue is exacerbated by the fact that, by the end of his six-year term, President Duterte had appointed all but three members of the Supreme Court. There was a sharp increase in favorable rulings for the Duterte administration, with high profile cases all being decided in his favor (Dressel, Inoue, and Bonoan 2023). With declines in constitutional practice under Duterte's populist leadership, the legal profession increasingly criticized the Court as being too deferential of the executive in high-profile political cases (e.g., burial in the national heroes cemetery of ousted president Ferdinand Marcos Sr.; affirmation of the arrest of Duterte critic Senator De Lima; declaration and extension of martial law in Mindanao; and the dismissal of a petition to compel the disclosure of Duterte's health condition in 2020) (Gatmaytan 2020; Gatmaytan 2023).

Meanwhile, the assertive presidency of Indonesia's Joko "Jokowi" Widodo (2014–24) has raised concerns about an increasingly deferential and "unheroic" Constitutional Court in a set of controversial decisions since 2020. These cases include the 2002 Komisi Pemberantasan Korupsi (KPK) Law; an omnibus bill on job creation, and the autonomy of Papua Province (Butt 2020). Concerns heightened with amendments to the Constitutional Court Law (2020) that adopted changes to the tenure and oversight of judges. Moreover, the fact that the populist president has come to dominate other branches of government involved in the nomination of justices in the mixed-appointment system that allows the executive, parliament, and the courts to each nominate three justices to the Constitutional Court has increased these concerns (Dressel and Susilo 2023).

The experiences of both the Philippines and Indonesia highlight the vulnerability of activist courts in Southeast Asia to executive encroachment. Civil society networks in both countries have been critical in moving the courts toward greater activism, for instance in questioning the constitutionality of laws and executive actions. However, the courts' increased political role also raises the stakes and invited attempts by other networks to influence decision-making. Against the background of strong executives, both courts have at times actively resisted and at other times fallen prey to traditional clientelist patterns of competing networks. Often anchored in loyalties, political and judicial networks enable these dynamics, as highlighted in highly contested appointment processes.

In the Philippines, the Judicial Bar Council (JBC) is tasked with the shortlisting of justices. Despite substantial public scrutiny over the selection process, the pressure of executive influence on JBC members has remained strong. Some presidents have interfered with the JBC nomination by using executive privilege to expand the list and appoint candidates generally perceived to lack character and integrity (Chua et al. 2012, 35). More so, with longstanding networks contributing to a relatively shallow pool of candidates, the networks become crucial to who is nominated and chosen, for instance when connecting an appointee to the president directly or via intermediaries (Gatmaytan and Magno 2011). Under the Duterte administration (2016–22), for example, there was an unprecedented increase in Supreme Court appointees from the president's own law school (Dressel, Inoue, and Bonoan 2023).

Likewise, the rise of executive control over parliament under President Joko Widodo (2009–24) has also meant that the boundaries between the branches of government are collapsing. Under Indonesia's multitrack system of appointments, the executive, parliament and judiciary appoint a third each of the Constitutional Court. However, the President's growing executive control over parliament effectively provides him with disproportionate power over court appointments. This has renewed concerns about the independence of the Constitutional Court, as highlighted in the controversial replacement of Constitutional Court Deputy Chief Justice Aswanto in 2022 by order of the House of Representatives (DPR) and the president. Aswanto's removal was widely seen as a response to his critical position on the Presidential flagship omnibus bill (Asshiddiqie 2023). Meanwhile, the fact that the current Chief Justice, Anwar Usman, has become the brother-in-law of the president has done little to alleviate these concerns.

Nevertheless, dynamics go beyond political interference. In the Philippines, journalistic accounts have highlighted how prominent lawyers may have exerted disproportionate influence on members of the Supreme Court. In one instance, a reconsideration of a case was described as having been possibly influenced by longstanding relationships and dynamics of seniority between counsel and certain justices (Vitug 2012, 118). Meanwhile, the arrests of two justices on the Constitutional Court in Indonesia for corruption and the investigation of another for ethics violations serve as reminders of the ever-present influence of political and private networks on high-level justices, including clientelist exchanges of desirable verdicts for money (Butt 2019a, 187) – a pattern long observed for lower level courts but now gradually moving up to formerly insulated higher courts.

In short, both legal mobilization from civil society and the competitive nature of oligarchic politics in both countries has offered justices considerable leeway to direct courts into a more activist path. With competing networks, and strong institutional safeguards post-authoritarian rule, competing networks were able to ensure varying interests in court appointments and decision-making. However, it is also clear that such an activist stance has invited political elites to seek influence over the courts – not just in the form of outright backlash, but rather by subtly activating relational networks to influence the work of justices in these institutions.

4.2 Politicization of the Judiciary: Thailand

The trajectory of the Thai Constitutional Court since 2006 has been quite different. Rather than being driven by an assertive independent bench, Thai judicial activism in areas of megapolitics reflects a quick politicization of the courts (Dressel 2010; Dressel and Tonsakulrungruang 2019). The centrality of the monarchy in the patronal–clientelist network has stifled the existence of alternative networks, skewing the decision-making of the constitutional court in political cases. From 1998 to 2016, the Constitutional Court decided on a total of 32 megapolitical cases. Studies have shown that dissent rates of individual judges in votes for/against government differ sharply across administrations depending on the political leanings of the government. Further, after the military coup in 2006, a mostly unanimous Constitutional Court consistently sided with administrations aligned with the monarchy and against those not traditionally seen as aligned with monarchical networks (Dressel and Tonsakulrungruang 2019).

The first decade of the Constitutional Court was tumultuous (Harding 2010). Established in 1998 by Thailand's 1997 "People's Constitution," the court was criticized by legal scholars for its conservatism during the administration of Prime Minister Thaksin Shinawatra (2001–06). The court was then dissolved by the 2006 military coup that revoked the 1997 constitution and replaced by a Constitutional Tribunal appointed by the military. It was reconstituted by the 2007 constitution with modified structures, powers, and bench composition. As political polarization and intra-elite conflict grew, the Constitutional Court and other Thai courts increasingly intervened in megapolitical areas and drew accusations from scholars of a lack of impartiality at best and outright political bias at worst (Tonsakulrungruang 2017).

Few would have predicted that trajectory. Envisioned as the guardian of the new liberal architecture and hub of a network of oversight agencies to strengthen rule-based governance (Leyland 2008; Harding 2010), the court enjoyed comparatively broad jurisdiction and – at least formally – solid safeguards for its independence. Originally composed of fifteen judges and now reduced to nine, the Constitutional Court bench is chosen through an elaborate system that allows for a professionally diverse group with each judge sitting for a single nonrenewable term.

A Thai military coup in 2006 and the new constitution adopted in 2007 significantly enlarged the political role of the court by involving it in the selection of senators and candidates to run independent agencies. It was allowed to propose laws directly to the House of Representatives. Most controversially, it was given the power to dissolve a political party if one of its leaders is found guilty of election fraud (Dressel 2009, 311–312).

The first manifestation of a new judicial assertiveness was the Constitutional Court's decision to annul the April 2006 general elections, even before the Courts' powers were expanded. The Thaksin government had called snap elections to counter growing public protests against allegations of corruption, disloyalty to the monarchy, and conflicts of interest. The monarchy-aligned opposition boycotted the election and filed a case to have it annulled. The court's decision was remarkable both in itself and in how it was handled. The unusually broad reasoning of the verdict of the Constitutional Court overruled the opinions of the Election Commission of Thailand (ECT), which many experts considered valid (Nelson 2006). There appeared to be an unusual degree of coordination between several courts. The Administrative Court had decided in April to cancel the rerun election of parliamentarians, in a blow to the Thaksin government. Meanwhile, the Constitutional Court annulled the general election and the Criminal Court brought cases against the Election Commissioners. Many legal observers believed the decisions favoring monarchical interests were linked to a speech in which the revered monarch had directly urged the courts to find a solution to the political impasse (see for an unofficial translation of the king's speech, *The Nation*, April 27, 2007).

In May 2007, the new Constitutional Tribunal dissolved the Thai Rak Thai (TRT) party and barred 111 of its members from public office for 5 years.[20] It was the first case heard by the military-appointed court, composed primarily of members who had been overtly critical of Thaksin. The decision came mere days after another royal speech to the Administrative Court in which the king urged the judges to find a solution to the political crisis ("I have the answer in my heart, but have no right to say it"). In finding the TRT and its allies Pattana Chart and Chart Thai guilty of election violations, the court effectively decapitated Thailand's largest and most popular political party, which had won landslide victories in 2001 and 2005. Not only was Thaksin Shinawatra now ineligible to run for office, but so was virtually anyone else who had risen with him. The same ruling unanimously acquitted the military-favored Democrat Party of all charges despite evidence of similar illicit activities. All of these decisions, highlight how judges respond to the signals from the monarchical networks, in which they find themselves embedded.

Two Constitutional Court cases in late 2008 suggested that the previous decisions were not aberrations. The first decision found Prime Minister

---

[20] Constitutional Tribunal Decision No. 3–5/2550, 2007.

Samak Sundaravej guilty of a conflict of interest for hosting a popular cooking show on TV.[21] The second dissolved the People's Power Party (PPP), the political successor to the TRT.[22] Both cases were heard after a landslide win by the PPP in the junta-organized general elections in December 2007 amidst a growing political stand-off between anti- and pro-Thaksin political camps. Again, the decisions had bold political implications. Prime Minister Samak was forced to resign for what many considered a minor abuse of power. His successor, Prime Minister Somchai, had to resign after PPP leader Yongyut Tiyapairat was found guilty of vote-buying. The decisions cleared the path for a Democrat-led government. Such court decisions have had profound effects on governance. The judges effectively destroyed Thailand's largest and most successful political party, forced the resignation of two prime ministers, and kept the pressure on the popular Thaksin to remain in exile.

Meanwhile, the courts' political bias continued. The expansion of the Court's political role via the military-drafted 2017 constitution (following the 2014 military coup and the royal succession in 2016), ushered in a string of cases. Several early decisions of the reconstituted Constitutional Court upheld the lèse-majesté law and sanctioned the pro-monarchy occupation of inner Bangkok (see Tonsakulrungruang 2016, 2017). High profile cases reached the court after the contested elections in 2019. The Court approved termination of the membership of all political parties, allowed General Prayuth Chan-ocha to run for Prime Minister by declaring that he was not a state officer, and dissolved Thaksin Shinawatra's proxy party, Thai Raksa Chart. In 2020, it dissolved the largest opposition party in parliament, the Future Forward Party (*Phak Anakhot Mai*), and banned its charismatic founder from parliament.

In 2021, the Constitutional Court also cleared the path for the Prayut Chan-ocha government to amend the 2017 constitution,[23] and further strengthened the hand of the government when it ruled to limit public protests that called for reform of the monarchy.[24] Reasoning that these protests intended to overthrow the state and the monarchy, the decision lent support to the growing legal crackdown and police repression of pro-democracy protesters (Haberkorn 2021; Tonsakulrungruang 2022).

Despite mass protests and growing calls for political reform and changes to the monarchy after the transition in 2016 to unpopular King Vajiralongkorn (Rama X), the Constitutional Court has continuously exhibited a pattern of decisions that have favored actors and parties associated with the military and

---

[21] Constitutional Court Decision No. 12–13/2551, 2008.

[22] Constitutional Court Decision No. 20/2551, 2008.

[23] Constitutional Court Decision No 4/2564 (2021).

[24] Constitutional Court Decision No 19/2564 (2021).

monarchical networks. Its growing involvement in megapolitical areas reflects its continuous politicization by traditional elites who have instrumentalized the judiciary – especially the Constitutional Court – to further their interests.

Growing ties between judicial and political networks has been the main driver of the politicization of the Thai Constitutional Courts. With constitutional reform reshaping the powers and composition of the Constitutional Court bench in 2006, 2007, and 2017, the court experienced changes in its membership due to its dissolution and the subsequent reduction of the bench from fifteen to nine members. These changes included a gradual replacement of law and political science experts with career bureaucrats tied to the state bureaucracy. Since 2006, the military-appointed Senate has appointed justices of the Court that have increasingly been recruited from within the ideological confines of the traditional military-monarchical network itself. This process has been actively facilitated by the Constitutional Court itself as it promoted ideological alignment between judges and political actors through joint workshops aimed at building personal relations, fostering ideological alignment among participants, and providing a pool for the recruitment of several future constitutional court judges (Dressel and Tonsakulrungruang 2019).

In sum, political networks have captured the decision-making of the Constitutional Court of Thailand. Their influence has created visible bias in the court's performance in politically charged cases, leaving the Court to act as an extended arm of government and the monarchy at large. As a result, the court has lost its ability to act as a neutral arbiter in political conflict. Moreover, its growing involvement in megapolitics directly reflects its ongoing capture by Thailand's traditional elite networks. Deeply hostile to majoritarian politics, such capture raises further questions over the role that the courts will play in times of growing democratic demands, as highlighted in the democratic opposition win in the 2023 general elections.

4.3 Judicial Restraint: Malaysia

The Malaysian Federal Court, formerly the Supreme Court, illustrates a trajectory in which a nominally independent court has traditionally decided to exert restraint and limit their engagement with megapolitics. However, this position has not always been tenable. In a historically one-party dominated system, political networks have traditionally managed to exert considerable influence over the judiciary. Nevertheless, an active legal complex has provided considerable accountability and support to the judiciary in the form of alternative networks. This has resulted in judicial restraint in megapolitical cases. From

1957 to 2018, the court has decided 102 cases, of which 85 percent were decided in favor the government, with limited dissent amongst members of the bench.

After the 1957 constitution, the Malaysian Supreme Court was quick to establish a path of strict literalism, self-imposed judicial restraint, and deference to legislative intent in political matters (Lee 1995, 2). In the first thirty-two years of independence, the court found only seven statutory provisions to be unconstitutional (three were reinstated on appeal, one was struck down by the Privy Council, and three were upheld). In cases involving fundamental rights, the court strictly adhered to a narrow reading of the constitution "within its own four walls" (see Thio 2005). Asked to adjudicate cases pitting an individual against the state – particularly concerning the Internal Security Act, which provided for detention without trial – the court often simply ruled that it had no jurisdiction. In one typical decision, then Chief Justice Raja Azlan Shah stated:

> Whether the impugned Act is "harsh and unjust" is a question of policy to be debated and decided by parliament, and therefore not meet for judicial determination. [. . .] Our courts ought not to enter this political thicket, even in such a worthwhile cause as the fundamental rights guaranteed by the Constitution. [. . .] Those who find fault with the wisdom or expediency of the impugned Act [. . .] normally must address themselves to the legislature and not the courts; they have their remedy at the ballot box (Loh Kooi Choon v. Government of Malaysia [1977] 2 MLJ 29).

Reflecting the widespread sentiment among judges and with the political realm providing the courts with little reason to intervene, the stance of the Malaysian Supreme Court was described as "judicial deference to legislative intent [and] pragmatic conservatism" (Thomas 1987, 98).

This pattern has persisted. Nevertheless, growing executive assertiveness and intra-elite tensions during the first Mahathir premiership (1982–2003) meant that the courts were occasionally drawn into high-level political and constitutional conflicts that involved the powers and immunity of Malaysian royalty (1983, 1992) and challenges to the political leadership (1988). Efforts to chart a more assertive, if not activist, path during these constitutional crises were short-lived. The gradual subjugation of the courts was evident after Lord President Tun Salleh Abas and five of his colleagues were removed at the height of the 1988 judicial crisis and the subsequent constitutional amendments limiting the court's powers (Khoo 1999), even amidst strong protests from the Malaysian Bar. The reputation of the courts was increasingly in doubt as they faced growing attacks against judicial independence and attempts to instrumentalize the courts in political cases, such as the 1998 sodomy trial against ousted Deputy Prime Minister Anwar Ibrahim (Lee and Foo 2017).

The post-Mahathir period, particularly the Abdullah Badawi premiership (2003–09), saw gradual efforts to rebalance executive–judicial relations. This included reforms to depoliticize the appointment process and tackle corruption within the courts. However, patterns of judicial decision-making hardly changed. Despite overturning Anwar's sodomy conviction in 2004, the Federal Court has avoided taking a clear position in highly contested religious cases,[25] to the point that constitutional questions of jurisdictional boundaries between Syariah and civil courts have not been fully resolved (Neo 2015; Moustafa 2018). Moreover, the court has ruled that the separation of powers doctrine, which delineates powers of each branch of government, is merely political and therefore insufficient to support a finding that a law is unconstitutional.[26] Then Chief Justice Tun Zaki Azmi (2008–10) even urged restraint and warned that judicial activism can be "a dangerous weapon in the hands of a too activist judge" (see "Practise Restraint, Judges Told," *New Straits Times*, July 31, 2010, p. 7).

Intensifying political competition that began in the elections of 2008 eventually ended six decades of political dominance by the Barisan Nasional (BN) party coalition in 2018. This transition provided new space for the courts as the influence of the traditional political networks weakened, although it has also meant that the Federal Court has become less predictable or even erratic. Certain cases suggest the occasional assertive judicial stance perhaps aimed at long-held ambitions for "constitutional redemption" (Tew 2016). In 2012, opposition leader Anwar Ibrahim was acquitted in the second trumped-up sodomy trial. There were rulings with an occasional nod to but with no real commitment to a "basic structure" doctrine, which prohibits parliament to change the core principles under the constitution. Accusations of politicized appointments to the bench, including post 2018, have continued. Under the Najib Razak's premiership (2009–18), political challenges for the government increased in parallel with efforts to tighten control over the highest court, primarily through the appointments of loyal Chief Justices, at times even beyond their term limits (e.g., see the much-criticized 2017 appointments of Chief Justice Tun Md Raus Sharif and Court of Appeal president Tan Sri Zulkefli Ahmad Makinudin as "additional judges" of the Federal Court, thereby effectively extending thereby effectively extending the tenure of judges perceived as loyal to the prime minister).

---

[25] Subashini Rajasingham v. Saravanan Thangathoray & other appeal [2008] 2 MLJ 147; see also Shamala Satiyaseelan v. Dr. Jeyaganesh C Mogarajah & Anor [2004] MLJ 648.

[26] Public Prosecutor v. Kok Wah Wah Kuan [2007] 6 CLJ 341.

To what extent Malaysia's shifting political terrain will force court leadership to chart a new path remains to be seen. The legal community has cautiously welcomed new appointments to the Federal Court. For the first time in the Court's history, gender parity was achieved 2018. Equally notable was the elevation of Maimun binti Tuan Mat (2019–present) as Malaysia's first female Chief Justice (Dressel and Inoue 2022). Under her tenure, the Federal Court has increasingly been thrown back into the limelight, forcing it to chart a careful path of its own institutional redemption in volatile times – for instance when ruling on the declaration of emergency during the COVID pandemic; the extent of press freedom (ruling that respected news outlet *Malaysiakini* was guilty of contempt of court in 2021), or the decision to deny the appeal of former PM Najib Razak in 2023 to have his graft conviction overturned (Shah 2020).

Whether this means that the pattern of self-imposed judicial restraint will hold is yet to be seen, considering how the Federal Court seeks to strike the right balance between institutional self-assertion and public accountability as illustrated in the case of GOJ-Harris Fathillah v Tan Sri Dato' Sri Haji Azam bin Baki (February 24, 2023). In this case, the Federal Court ruled that while judges may be held accountable for criminal offences, the sole authority to investigate and discipline members of the judiciary remains with the Chief Justice, thereby ensuring judicial independence. It is worth noting that the Malaysian Bar supported the independence of the courts from political interference in their opinion, by acting as amicus curiae in the case.

It is clear that the judicial behavior of the Federal Court remains shaped by networks across the judiciary. Historical single-party dominance allowed political networks to exert influence over the appointments, promotions, and selection of judges in high-profile cases. Relatively inexperienced high court judge Augustine Paul was assigned to preside over the sodomy and corruption cases of opposition leader Anwar Ibrahim. Despite questionable evidence, the judge found him guilty (Trowell 2015). Judge Augustine Paul was eventually appointed to the Federal Court bench, mere months before retirement. Dynamics like these have far-reaching consequences for the professionalism, independence, and legitimacy of the judiciary. At the same time, professional networks within and outside the judiciary have mounted successful challenges to these practices of judicial clientelism and patronage, aided by an internal judicial *esprit de corps* and close ties between judges and the Malaysian Bar (Weiss 2006; Harding and Whiting 2012). Their successful advocacy for the establishment of a judicial appointments commission in 2009 has produced a different pool of superior court judges in terms of qualifications, gender, and ethnicity over the last decade.

In turn, this has provided for new leadership (e.g., CJs Malanjum, Maimun Tuan Mat) and an altered Federal Court bench to emerge after 2018.

In sum, as the dominant political-clientelist settlement has begun to unravel in an increasingly competitive environment, with the loss of single-party dominance, Malaysian traditional political networks have also lost influence over the judiciary. The more competitive environment has allowed professional–legal networks to increasingly replace and challenge traditional networks. As a result, the pattern of self-imposed restraint is eroding just as the court strategically reasserts itself within an increasingly volatile environment. This may have consequences for a string of high-profile criminal cases against present and past UMNO leaders (e.g., Najib, Zahid Hamidi, Muhyiddin Yassin).

4.4 A Muted Approach: Singapore

The trajectory of the Singapore Supreme Court is marked by both limited judicial independence and limited engagement in megapolitics. Having never experienced an institutional rupture and having consistently operated within the soft authoritarian rule of the PAP, the court exemplifies the limits of judicial autonomy. In a strong clientelist-hegemonic environment, the executive is dominant, resulting in the breakdown of the separations of powers in practice. Independent networks are stifled, thereby weakening the linkages between judges and the legal complex. This pattern can also be found in authoritarian countries such as Cambodia and Myanmar and socialist countries such as Vietnam and Laos, further exacerbated by weaker institutional capacities of courts in these countries.

Singapore's legal system is regularly ranked among the best in the world. The government has gone to great lengths to stress the role of the courts in ensuring good governance (Thio 2012; Neo 2017). Nevertheless, serious questions have been raised about their impartiality and independence, particularly in politically sensitive cases (Littlemore 1998; Worthington 2001; International Bar Association 2008; Rajah 2012). Against the backdrop of the state's authoritarian use of the law that has curtailed civil and political liberties, the stifling of political opposition, and the entrenchment of the ruling party, Worthington (2003: 133) notes that the "separation of powers is observed in work only; the legislature and the judiciary are disenfranchised by the executive, and the legal profession has no capacity to challenge or even advise the executive." Considerable government control and pervasive corporatist ideology have resulted in the courts showing few signs of activism and having virtually no engagement with megapolitics.

Since the Singapore Supreme Court was founded in 1957, it has exercised its judicial review powers cautiously (it has reviewed 79 cases, and only in 27.8 percent of these cases have the applicants won). Virtually none of its cases address substantive constitutional or political issues. The five-year reviews of legal developments published by the Singapore Academy of Law do not provide a single chapter on constitutional and administrative law, as the Chief Justice has pointed out (Keong 2010, 473). While this partly reflects a lack of open contestation in a tightly controlled political system, it also illustrates government efforts to exert subtle control over the courts, particularly the Supreme Court. Measures to exert control include the removal of external review (appeals to the Privy Council ceased in 1994); legislation to curtail court sentencing prerogatives; direct influence over the terms of appointments through the exercise of executive discretion in appointing Supreme Court judges (many of whom are linked to the PAP inner circle); rotation of judges through legal service positions; lack of tenure for many judges; and extension of contracts at the Supreme Court beyond legal retirement age at the will of the prime minister. These practices are in addition to the tight regulation of judges through corporatist control of gateways to the bench, such as the Singapore Law Society and institutions of legal education (e.g., law schools; training academies such as the Singapore Judicial College). Unsurprisingly, courts have done little to address core political issues.

This is not to say that Singaporean courts are irrelevant. The government has been careful to support the image of a professional and efficient judiciary. Supreme Court commercial decisions retain the confidence of the international business community. While there is evidence of judicial review exercised in economic cases, the dynamics in politically sensitive cases can be very different (Chua and Haynie 2016). For instance, in defamation cases against prominent opposition members (e.g., Joshua Benjamin Jeyaretnam; Francis Seow; Chee Soo Juan), the courts have deviated abruptly from long-held principles of English law, and damages awarded in these cases are drastically different from the awards in nonpolitical cases (see Worthington 2003, 126).

The blatant use of the courts for political purposes may have caused difficulties in filling the Supreme Court bench, with some judges accepting appointments only on the condition that they do not hear political cases (Worthington 2001, 516). Some judges appear to support the corporatist communal ideology in seeking to keep political conflict out of the courts. For instance, in a 2010 speech Chief Justice Chan Sek Keong stated that the courts should not be seen as a "first line of defense against administrative abuses of power but as a support to Parliament and the Executive itself" as they articulate "clear rules and principles by which government may abide and conform to the rule of law" (Keong 2010, 480). Hence, only on rare occasions has the Singapore Supreme Court engaged in megapolitical areas (e.g., cases against opposition members). In cases where it has done so, it has often acted at the insistence of the executive (see cases against *Financial Times, International Herald Tribune, Bloomberg* and *Asian Wall Street Journal*).

The Singapore Supreme Court demonstrates how courts are deeply embedded in one-party dominated political systems and the difficulty of judicial assertiveness where the executive remains dominant. However, with little change in its judicial pattern over time, the Singaporean case also highlights weak relational linkages across the legal complex. With only sixty-six Supreme courts judges appointed since independence, the top judiciary has remained small. Moreover, what is notable is "the existence of invisible barriers within Singapore's legal landscape, and in particular the absence of a lawyer-judge nexus" (Rajah 2012, 159). This means weak linkages between bench and bar, which has left the judiciary and lawyers poorly aligned on issues of rights and has also promoted a "significant concentration or collaboration between the judiciary and the executive" (Jayasuriya 1999, 173). State suppression of university radicals in the 1960s and 1970s, meanwhile, also diminished critical voices from academia. PM Lee's intervention to bring down the state's legal-administrative apparatus on Singapore's Law Society and its outspoken members in 1987/88 has meant that for more than three decades, the Law Society stayed out of the public domain. Altogether, this has weakened critical voices on Singapore's judiciary and legal system, and prevented any meaningful role in the appointment process of judges (Rajah 2012).

Hence, it is unsurprising that efforts to chart a new path for the courts have proved difficult. The Court has traditionally shied away from ruling on the long-standing issue of a "basic structure doctrine," as many academic experts on the Singapore Constitution have called for (Harding 2016). In a 2017 decision, the Court once again quickly retreated from the issue after the government argued that such doctrine would block "progressive changes."[27] Unlike in the past, however, this time the Court engaged critically with the proposal and discussed what it would mean for constitutional doctrine (Neo 2018). Growing political in-fighting within the PAP as the party moves away from the founding Lee dynasty may yet open new avenues for the judiciary. A 2022 Court of Appeal decision to overturn the previous High Court ruling

---

[27] *Ravi s/o Madasamy v Attorney-General and other matters ("Ravi s/o Madasamy")*, [2017] SGHC 163.

against three members of the opposition Workers Party in matters of local governance was widely noted for its more nuanced treatment of the opposition, even as the court still ruled that its members could be liable for damages over possible gross negligence.[28]

Singapore's courts are thus best described as "muted" on megapolitics as the political sphere is largely de-judicialized. As a result, the government has been able to project and maintain a public image of court impartiality, professionalism, and efficiency in non-political cases, thereby projecting the image of a leading regional trade hub anchored in the rule of law. The dynamic is based on the close personal and ideological ties between political and the court elites as well as the weak ties between the judiciary and the legal profession on issues of rights in a tightly controlled political system. Hence, unchallenged by independent judicial networks, a dual system of justice has emerged in which political and 'ordinary' cases receive different treatment, revealing the complexities of the relationship between judicialization and governance in Singapore. It combines state legalism with an efficient judiciary more accountable to the executive than the public in a pattern that has become popular for other authoritarian states in the region to try to emulate.

4.5 Judicialization and the Influence of Networks

In sum, the previous case studies have highlighted variations in the judicialization trend. These patterns can be seen as a confluence of ideational, institutional, and structural features that range from the scope and powers of the courts; legal ideational legacies of justice institutions; and the political context in which a court system operates. In short, both law and politics come into play when seeking to understand patterns in political cases exhibited by high courts in Southeast Asia (Kapiszewski, Silverstein, and Kagan 2013b; Roux 2018b).

If there is a common thread across the diverse judicial dynamics in the region, it is that purely legal analysis is often insufficient. Neither is it helpful to focus on formal institutions alone. Instead, as our case studies suggest, more attention needs to be directed to the informal nature of politics in Southeast Asian countries and the pressures exerted on court systems by deeply ingrained oligarchic, clientelistic, and patronage-based political practices, including hegemonic one party dominance. These powerful informal forces can be studied through the lens of judicial networks. Such networks can provide pathways for

---

[28] AHTC case; www.channelnewsasia.com/singapore/ahtc-case-court-appeal-finds-gross-negligence-payments-process-3056931

political influence through personal loyalties and clientelist exchanges or broadly undermine judicial independence and rule-based practices between judges and political and private actors through material and nonmaterial social ties (Dressel, Sanchez Urribarri, and Stroh 2017).

The role of networks can have negative consequences. The impeachment scandals of Chief Justices Corona (2012) in the Philippines and Akil Mochtar (2013) in Indonesia both show how informal dynamics might lead to corruption. However, informal dynamics often extend well beyond the corruption of judges (Dressel 2018). As the Thai case study shows, political elites have traditionally built close connections with the courts, facilitated by the patronal pyramid centered on the Thai monarchy (Mérieau 2016). Similarly, in Singapore, while the courts are generally perceived as efficient, close personal and ideological ties to the political establishment (the PAP) engender loyalties in cases that challenge the regime. That pattern is explicit in Vietnam and Laos, where socialist state ideology allows the party to direct outcomes in politically sensitive cases (Gillespie 2007). As shown in Malaysia, control of judicial appointments is equally critical, particularly at the high court level. It allows the regime to control the outcomes of cases despite occasional setbacks in lower courts. These dynamics are also visible in more competitive-oligarchic settings, such as the Philippines, although the presidential term limit under its constitution has brought greater factionalization to the bench in terms of votes in high-profile cases (Dressel, Inoue, and Bonoan 2023). By contrast, military-authoritarian regimes (e.g., Myanmar) have often used direct interference and threats of violence. This was evident in the removal of judges from Myanmar's highest court, the Constitutional Tribunal (Marti 2015). And in Cambodia, pressure, intimidation, and violence have been used against judges (International Bar Association 2015).

Not all networks impact the judiciary negatively. The gradual professionalization of judges and an active legal complex can protect against corruption and undue influence by advocating for greater accountability and institutionalization of practices. The activism and pressure by the Malaysian Bar have been critical in establishing a Judicial Appointments Commission and encouraging whistleblowers to come forward. In the Philippines, members of civil society organizations and the bar association regularly offer opinions about the shortlist for judicial appointments prepared by the Judicial and Bar Council (JBC), as well as file petitions to question executive prerogatives and controversial laws. These groups have also been critical in drawing public attention to the constitutional implications of the questionable removal of CJ Sereno in 2018. Nevertheless, few countries in Southeast Asia have such a vibrant and well-organized legal complex. In Indonesia, the legal profession is more fragmented, weakening its political role. Even in Malaysia, broad changes to the profession (e.g., greater inclusion of Islamic lawyers; widening gaps between large and small law firms) have also brought new impediments to collective action (Harding and Whiting 2012). Similarly, political polarization can affect the legal complex, as shown in sharp divisions between law schools, legal fraternities, and members of the Bar during the Corona and Sereno impeachments in the Philippines.

Finally, it must be recognized that the judiciary is a strategic actor with considerable agency. This is true both at the institutional court and the individual judge level. While courts are principally reactive institutions (they respond to cases brought before them), the court leadership can shape the trajectory of justice institutions by working with allies, such as NGOs or bilateral or international organizations engaged in judicial reform. At the individual judge level, ascension to the highest court means that many justices have learned to navigate through the pervasive practices of patronage and clientelism in the courts and beyond. Hence, studying the ability of judges to marshal personal loyalties and networks on and off the bench is critical to a deeper understanding of the patterns described in these case studies.

5 Conclusion and Outlook

This Element has drawn attention to the gradual revival of and occasional backlash against the judiciary in Southeast Asia in the last quarter century as part of the global trend toward the "judicialization of politics," and its contemporary challenges. Highlighting the historical-institutional roots and political patterns the judiciary in the region exhibits, I argued that this diverse region may be best understood in terms of hybrid-clientelist regimes, where formal and informal institutions are strongly interwoven and informality permeates institutional practice. Variations in clientelar patterns affect what role networks can play in influencing the judiciary. In competitive-oligarchic settings, such as the Philippines and Indonesia, competing networks will seek to influence the judiciary, driving dissent, and propelling greater activism. This is compounded by institutional empowerment of the courts. By contrast, the patronal-clientelist regime in Thailand facilitates the capture of the court by a single network. Meanwhile historically hegemonic settings, such as Malaysia and Singapore, limit the role of competing networks, though resulting to varying degrees in outcomes ranging from muteness to restraint in megapolitical cases.

Informality and relational dynamics have received scant attention in judicial politics scholarship. This is particularly true for the role of informal judicial networks that operate on and off the bench. Showing how judicial networks operate across diverse institutional-clientelar settings transcends the traditional focus on regime types in explaining judicial dynamics and outcomes. It also draws attention to the judicial actors themselves – how their motivations are constituted, the type of broader constraints at play, and how judges navigate the tension between law, politics, and informality in these settings. Thus, the relational perspective offers a deeper understanding of judicial dynamics – one that is grounded in shared realities across this complex region.

What should be clear is that Southeast Asia has much to offer from empirical and theoretical perspectives. The unusual diversity of political, legal, and cultural systems and the sharp differences in judicial behavior and performance exhibited by the judiciary in the region offers considerable challenges to the study of judicial behavior and the performance of judges and judicial institutions.

As such, the region provides a unique testing ground for existing theories, but also urges us to re-engage conceptually and empirically with the dynamics of judicial behavior and judicial performance. A relational–sociological perspective that includes the varied roles that a judges' network plays is a fruitful way to engage in this much-needed conversation – one lacking in comparative judicial politics scholarship to date. For example, much remains to be studied about the role of women's networks in the judiciary. The emergence of a strong female judge network in the Philippines prompts questions about the factors supporting such developments in the absence of similar successful networks in the region. More specifically: What brings them together, where do they engage, and how the feminist perspective might influence decision-making?

The issues highlighted here are not unique to Southeast Asia. Many of the patterns of informality that have been described are common to states in the Global South and can even be found in judiciaries in the developed world. This is evident in the powerful role that educational and ideological networks play in the selection of clerks and appointees to the US Supreme Court (Scherer and Miller 2009; Katz and Stafford 2010), or the effects of networks operating within and outside international courts (Harlow and Rawlings 2007; Dothan 2018). Nevertheless, the effects of informal networks are often more potent in states where institutions are weak. In the absence of accountability structures, the perception of capture and/or influence of the judicial institutions by networks questions the legitimacy of the judicial system itself. While personal relationships are an integral part of any society and work environment, they become highly consequential in settings where institutions lack autonomy and regularly struggle with disproportionate influence from small, yet powerful elite actors.

From this vantage point, the relational perspective ultimately draws attention to what Ginsburg (2003, 20) once described as one of the most important sociolegal questions of our time, namely how "political systems can transform from one governed by personalistic forms of authority towards one in which the rule of law prevails." Southeast Asia tells a cautionary tale in this respect. While the colonial state-building project has provided the foundation for many modern institutions, including those of the judiciary, this failed to result in the dominance of impersonal rule. Despite rapid modernization, many institutions remain deeply embedded in primordial patterns of loyalty, friendship, ethnicity, and religion. Political power remains significantly anchored in personalistic rule, patronage, and the mobilization of patron–client ties. The result is a degree of "isomorphic mimicry" – a pattern where institutions look like those known from the West with actors within them mimicking practices and performing similar roles and rituals, but in which their performances and intentions are often very different (Andrews, Pritchett, and Woolcock 2017).

This prompts questions about the prospects for greater judicial independence and professionalism, and by extension, how the rule of law can gain hold in the region. These questions have risen to prominence because of the puzzling diversity in judicial performance across the region as well as the rise of illiberal governance by increasingly authoritarian and populist regimes over the last decade. As highlighted by developments in the Philippines, Thailand, and Indonesia, the judiciary can occasionally be used as a tool in broader efforts to dismantle the constitutional order. Its instrumentalization is often part of a set of authoritarian innovations in the region (Curato and Fossati 2020), fostered by deep entanglements of judges with anti-democratic politicians, either as part of relational patronage ties or ideological commitments to the anti-democratic order born out of networks. From this vantage point, it is clear that judges are not mere victims. They may be complicit in helping shape the authoritarian revival in the region.

It must also be acknowledged that despite the influence of international discourse on the rule of law shaping the self-perception of the judiciary over the last quarter century, the growing success of authoritarian legalism in the region has meant that "thin" notions of the rule of law (or those based on ideas of "order over law") are seen by many political elites as viable alternatives to rule of law ideas associated with the liberal model in the West. This is particularly the case in settings where traditional elites have come under pressure from majoritarian-electoral processes, such as Thailand.

The Singaporean models provide much appeal to powerholders in the region. Unlike its Chinese counterpart, however, the judiciary in Singapore is widely known for its professionalism and independence in the majority of cases, except for those in the political sphere (Worthington 2003). Akin to Fraenkel's "dual state" in which two legal spheres operate side-by-side, thus system has allowed Singapore to successfully portray itself as a rule of law state with an independent judiciary while maintaining its selective political order. This public image is harder to achieve for the judiciary in Vietnam and Laos under the state principle of democratic-centralism (Hurst 2020).

The outcome of this ongoing constitutional contestation may be difficult to predict but judicial actors and the legal complex will clearly play an important part in the battle over the rule of law and constitutionalism in the region. While it is true that judicial actors have traditionally been closely aligned with the ruling elites and their state-building project, educational and global changes have imbued judges with new ideas and embedded them in wider regional networks. As a result, high courts and individual judges have been at the forefront of new initiatives to strengthen the independence and professionalism of the judiciary in the region (e.g., Beijing Statement of the Principles of Judicial Independence of the Judiciary in the Lawasia Region). In the worst of times, however, they have also become instrumental in the protection of narrow elite interests and may have even supported corrupt activities.

These contradictions invite greater anthropological and sociological work on the "lifeworlds" of these critical actors. As argued, a relational perspective to judicial behavior invites a closer look at the judicial actors, their networks, and the complex social reality that they inhabit. In doing so, it helps reveal the contextual dynamic tension that many judges find themselves in: between the law and professional expectations versus social relations and obligations they are tied to. How they disentangle themselves from the ties that bind largely determines how decisions are made and if judicial institutions are able to operate autonomously without being captured by political and private interests.

These insights have practical implications. Judicial reforms have often failed and access to justice has remained limited, possibly due to the traditional reform focus on institutional design. As highlighted in this Element, however, transforming judicial performance and behavior is not just an issue of institutional change. It depends on the interplay between formal and informal rules. Institutional change in the form of constitutional change often provides a window for broader engagement. Hence, focusing on the role of informal judicial networks of actors, their ideas, and how they spread is crucially important to understand how reforms can be supported. It is a reminder for those in charge of governance reform to think more clearly about building alliances and sustaining reform momentum against internal and external resistance in institutions such as the judiciary. The relational approach is critical to this endeavor.

References

Ackerman, Bruce. 1997. "The Rise of World Constitutionalism." *Virginia Law Review* 83:771–797.

Amnesty International. 2021. Philippines: Surge in Killings of Lawyers and Judges Shows Justice System "in Deadly Danger." www.amnesty.org/en/latest/news/2021/03/philippines-surge-killings-lawyers/.

Andrews, Matt, Lant Pritchett, and Michael Woolcock. 2017. *Building State Capability*. Oxford: Oxford University Press.

Appleby, Gabrielle, and Andrew Lynch, eds. 2021. *The Judge, the Judiciary and the Court: Individual, Collegial and Institutional Judicial Dynamics in Australia*. Cambridge: Cambridge University Press.

Armytage, Livingston. 2011. "Judicial Reform in Asia: Case Study of ADB's Experience: 1990–2007." *Hague Journal on the Rule of Law* 3:70–105.

Armytage, Livingston. 2012. *Reforming Justice. A Journey to Fairness in Asia*. Cambridge: Cambridge University Press.

Aspinall, Edward, and Ward Berenschot. 2019. *Democracy for Sale Elections, Clientelism, and the State in Indonesia*. Ithaca: Cornell University Press.

Asshiddiqie, Jimly. 2023. "Can a Constitutional Court Judgment be Changed? Newly Installed Judge Faces Ethics Council." University of Melbourne, accessed April 24, 2023. https://indonesiaatmelbourne.unimelb.edu.au/can-a-constitutional-court-judgment-be-changed-newly-installed-judge-faces-ethics-council/.

Bailey, Michael A., and Forrest Maltzman. 2011. *The Constrained Court: Law, Politics and the Decisions Justices Make*. Princeton: Princeton University Press.

Basabe-Serrano, Santiago. 2015. "Informal Institutions and Judicial Independence in Paraguay, 1954–2011." *Law & Policy* 37 (4):350–378.

Baum, Lawrence. 1994. "What Judges Want: Judges' Goals and Judicial Behavior." *Political Research Quarterly* 47 (3):749–768.

Baum, Lawrence. 2006. *Judges and Their Audiences: A Perspective on Judicial Behavior*. Princeton: Princeton University Press.

Baum, Lawrence. 2010. "Motivation and Judicial Behavior: Expanding the Scope of Inquiry." In *The Psychology of Judicial Decision Making*, edited by David E. Klein, and Gregory Mitchell, 3–26. Oxford: Oxford University Press.

Blichner, Lars Chr. , and Anders Molander. 2008. "Mapping Juridification." *European Law Journal* 14 (1):36–54.

Bourchier, David. 1999. "Magic Memos, Collusion and Judges with Attitudes: Notes on the Politics of Law in Contemporary Indonesia." In *Law, Capitalism and Power in Asia*, edited by Kanishka Jayasuriya, 233–252. London: Routledge.

Box-Steffensmeier, Janet M., Dino P. Christenson, and Claire Levitt. 2016. "Judicial Networks." In *The Oxford Handbook of Political Networks*, edited by Alexander H. Montgomery, Jennifer Nicoll Victor, and Mark Lubell, 491–515. Oxford: Oxford University Press.

Brocheux, Pierre, and Daniel Hemery. 2009. *Indochina. An Ambiguous Colonization, 1858–1954*. London: University of California Press.

Butt, Simon. 2015. *The Constitutional Court and Democracy in Indonesia*. Leiden: Brill Nijhoff.

Butt, Simon. 2019a. "Indonesia's Anti-corruption Courts and the Persistence of Judicial Culture." In *The Politics of Court Reform: Judicial Change and Legal Culture in Indonesia*, edited by Melissa Crouch, 151–173. Cambridge: Cambridge University Press.

Butt, Simon. 2019b. "The Indonesian Constitutional Court: Reconfiguring Decentralization for Better or Worse?" *Asian Journal of Comparative Law* 14 (1):147–174.

Butt, Simon. 2020. "The 2020 Constitutional Court Law Amendments: A 'Gift' to Judges?" *Indonesia at Melbourne Blog*, September 3. https://indonesiaat melbourne.unimelb.edu.au/the-2020-constitutional-court-law-amendments-a-gift-to-judges/.

Butt, Simon, and Thimothy Lindsey. 2010. "Judicial Mafia: The Courts and State Illegality in Indonesia." In *The State and Illegality in Indonesia*, edited by Edward Aspinall, and Gerry van Klinken, 189–214. Leiden: Brill.

Carothers, Thomas. 2003. *Promoting the Rule of Law Abroad : The Problem of Knowledge*. Washington, DC: Carnegie Endowment for International Peace.

Chang, Wen-Chen, Li-ann Thio, Kevin YL Tan, and Jiunn-rong Yeh. 2014. *Constitutionalism in Asia. Cases and Materials*. Oxford: Hart.

Cheesman, Nick. 2011. "How an Authoritarian Regime in Burma Used Special Courts to Defeat Judicial Independence." *Law & Society Review* 45 (4): 801–830.

Cheesman, Nick. 2015. *Opposing the Rule of Law: How Myanmar's Courts Make Law and Order*. Cambridge: Cambridge University Press.

Chen, Albert H. Y. 2018. "Constitutional Courts in Asia: Western Origins and Asian Practices." In *Constitutional Courts in Asia: A Comparative Perspective*, edited by Albert H. Y. Chen, and Andrew James Harding, 1–32. Cambridge: Cambridge University Press.

Chen, Albert H. Y. 2010. "Pathways of Western Liberal Constitutional Development in Asia: A Comparative Study of Five Major Nations." *I Con* 8 (4):849–884.

Chen, Albert H. Y., and Andrew James Harding, eds. 2018. *Constitutional Courts in Asia*. Cambridge: Cambridge University Press.

Chua, Lynette J., and Stacia L. Haynie. 2016. "Judicial Review of Executive Power in the Singaporean Context, 1965–2012." *Journal of Law and Courts* 4 (1):43–64.

Chua, Yvonne T., Booma B. Cruz, Ma. Gisela Ordenes-Cascolan et al. 2012. "Political Economy Analysis of Judicial Appointments in the Philippines." *VERA Files*, 1–94.

Ciencia Jr. , Alejandro N. 2012. "From Judicialization to Politicization of the Judiciary: The Philippine Case." In *The Judicialization of Politics in Asia*, edited by Björn Dressel, 117–138. New York: Routledge.

Croissant, Aurel. 2010. "Provisions, Practices and Performances of Constitutional Review in Democratizing East Asia." *Pacific Review* 23 (5): 549–578.

Crouch, Harold. 1986. "Patrimonialism and Military Rule in Indonesia." In *The State and Development in the Third World*, edited by A. Kohli, 242–258., Princeton: Princeton University Press.

Crouch, Melissa, ed. 2021. *Women and the Judiciary in the Asia-Pacific*. Cambridge: Cambridge University.

Cruz, Isagani A., and Cynthia Cruz-Datu. 2000. *Res Gestae*. Manila: Rex Book Store.

Cunningham, Charles Henry. 1912. *The Audiencia in the Spanish Colonies as Illustrated by the Audiencia of Manila (1583–1800)*. Berkeley: University of California Press.

Curato, Nicole, and Diego Fossati. 2020. "Authoritarian Innovations: Crafting Support for a Less Democratic Southeast Asia." *Democratization* 27 (6): 1006–1020.

Day, Tony. 2002. *Fluid Iron: State Formation in Southeast Asia*. Honolulu: University of Hawai'i Press.

De Visser, Maartje. 2016. "We All Stand together: The Role of the Association of Asian Constitutional Courts and Equivalent Institutions in Promoting Constitutionalism." *Asian Journal of Law and Society* 3 (1):105–134.

Deinla, Imelda. 2014. "Public Support and Judicial Empowerment of the Philippine Supreme Court." *Contemporary Southeast Asia: A Journal of International and Strategic Affairs* 36 (1):128–158.

Desierto, Desiree A. 2015. "Judicial Independence: Evidence from the Philippine Supreme Court (1970–2003)." In *The Political Economy of*

Governance, edited by Norman Schofield, and Gonzalo Caballero, 41–57. Cham: Springer International.

Dick, Howard, and Timothy Lindsey. 2002. *Corruption in Asia: Rethinking the Governance Paradigm*. Annandale NSW: The Federation Press.

Domingo, Pilar. 2004. "Judicialization of Politics or Politicization of the Judiciary? Recent Trends in Latin America." *Democratization* 11 (1): 104–126.

Domingo, Pilar, and Rachel Sieder. 2001. *Rule of Law in Latin America : The International Promotion of Judicial Reform*. London: University of London Institute of Latin American Studies.

Donovan, Dolores A. 1993. "Cambodia: Building a Legal System from Scratch." *The International Lawyer* 27 (2):445–454.

Dothan, Shai. 2018. "The Motivations of Individual Judges and How They Act as a Group." *German Law Journal* 19 (7):2165–2188.

Dressel, Björn. 2009. "Thailand's Elusive Quest for a Constitutional Equilibrium, 1997–2007." *Contemporary Southeast Asia* 31 (2):296–325.

Dressel, Björn. 2010. "Judicialization of Politics or Politicization of the Judiciary? Considerations from Recent Events in Thailand." *The Pacific Review* 23 (5):671–691.

Dressel, Björn, ed. 2012. *The Judicialization of Politics in Asia*. New York: Routledge.

Dressel, Björn. 2018. "The Informal Dimension of Constitutional Politics in Asia: Insights from the Philippines and Indonesia." In *Constitutional Courts in Asia*, edited by Albert H.Y. Chen, and Andrew James Harding, 60–86. Cambridge: Cambridge University Press.

Dressel, Björn, and Fakhridho Susilo. 2023. "Presidential Democracies." In *Routledge Handbook of Asian Parliaments*, edited by Po Jen Yap, and Rehan Abeyratne, 82–99. London: Routledge.

Dressel, Björn, and Khemthong Tonsakulrungruang. 2019. "Coloured Judgement? The Work of the Thai Constitutional Court, 1998–2016." *Journal of Contemporary Asia* 49 (1):1–23.

Dressel, Björn, and Marcus Mietzner. 2012. "The Judicialization of Electoral Politics in Asia: A Tale of Two Courts." *Governance* 25 (3):391–414.

Dressel, Björn, and Tomoo Inoue. 2018a. "Informal Networks and Judicial Decisions: Insights from the Philippines Supreme Court, 1986–2015." *International Political Science Review* 39 (5):616–633.

Dressel, Björn, and Tomoo Inoue. 2018b. "Megapolitical Cases before the Constitutional Court of Indonesia since 2004: An Empirical Study." *Constitutional Review* 4 (2):157–187.

Dressel, Björn, and Tomoo Inoue. 2022. "Politics and the Federal Court of Malaysia, 1960–2018: An Empirical Investigation." *Asian Journal of Law and Society* 9 (1):26–58.

Dressel, Björn, Raul Sanchez Urribarri, and Alexander Stroh. 2017. "The Informal Dimension of Judicial Politics: A Relational Perspective." *Annual Review of Law and Social Science* 13:413–430.

Dressel, Björn, Raul Sanchez Urribarri, and Alexander Stroh. 2018. "Courts and Informal Networks: Towards a Relational Perspective on Judicial Politics beyond Western Democracies." *International Political Science Review* 39 (5): 573–584.

Dressel, Björn, Tomoo Inoue, and Cristina Bonoan. 2023. "Justices and Political Loyalties: An Empirical Investigation of the Supreme Court of the Philippines, 1987–2020." *Law and Social Inquiry*:1–25.

Dworkin, Ronald. 1990. *A Bill of Right for Britain*. London: Chatto and Windus.

Elson, Robert E. 1999. "International Commerce, the State and Society: Economic and Social Change." In *The Cambridge History of Southeast Asia*, edited by Nicholas Tarling, 127–189. Cambridge: Cambridge University Press.

Engel, David M. 1978. *Code and Custom in a Thai Provincial Court: The Interaction of Formal and Informal Systems of Justice*. Tucson: University of Arizona Press.

Engel, David M., and Jaruwan Engel. 2010. *Tort, Custom, and Karma: Globalization and Legal Consciousness in Thailand*. Palo Alto: Stanford University Press.

Epp, Charles R. 1998. *The Rights Revolution: Lawyers, Activists and Supreme Courts in Comparative Perspective*. Chicago: University of Chicago Press.

Epstein, Lee, and Jack Knight. 1998. *The Choices Justices Make*. Washington, DC: CQ Press.

Epstein, Lee, and Keren Weinshall. 2021. *The Strategic Analysis of Judicial Behavior, Cambridge Elements: Law, Economics, and Politics*. Cambridge: Cambridge University Press.

Erdmann, Gero, and Ulf Engel. 2006. "Neopatrimonialism Revisited – beyond a Catch-All Concept." *GIGA Working Papers*:16.

Escresa, Laarni, and Nuno Garoupa. 2012. "Judicial Politics in Unstable Democracies: The Case of the Philippine Supreme Court, an Empirical Analysis 1986–2010." *Asian Journal of Law and Economics* 3 (1):1–37.

Feeley, Malcom, and Edward L. Rubin. 1998. *Judicial Policy Making and the Modern State: How the Courts Reformed America's Prisons*. Cambridge: Cambridge University Press.

Fifield, Russell H. 1983. "Southeast Asia as a Regional Concept." *Southeast Asian Journal of Social Science* 11 (2):1–14.

Fischman, Joshua B. 2013. "Interpreting Circuit Court Voting Patterns: A Social Interactions Framework." *The Journal of Law, Economics, and Organization* 31 (4):808–842.

Fischman, Joshua B. 2015. "Interpreting Circuit Court Voting Patterns: A Social Interactions Framework." *The Journal of Law, Economics, and Organization* 31 (4):808–842.

Friedman, Lawrence M. 2006. "Judging the Judges: Some Remarks on the Way Judges Think and the Way Judges Act." In *Norms and the Law*, edited by John N. Drobak, 139–160. Cambridge: Cambridge University Press.

Fuhse, Jan. 2015. "Theorizing Social Networks: The Relational Sociology of and around Harrison White." *International Review of Sociology* 25 (1):15–44.

Furnivall, John Sydendam. 1956 (1948). *Colonial Policy and Practice: A Comparative Study of Burma and the Netherlands India*. New York: New York University Press.

Gatmaytan, Dante. 2023. *Emergencies and Executions: The Erosion of the Rule of Law under the Duterte Regime*. Manila: UP Law Centre.

Gatmaytan, Dante B. 2020. "Judicial Review and Emergencies in Post-Marcos Philippines." *Constitutionalism under Extreme Conditions: Law, Emergency, Exception* 82:41–62.

Gatmaytan, Dante B., and Cielo Magno. 2011. "Averting Diversity: A Review of Nominations and Appointments to the Philippine Supreme Court (1988–2008)." *Asian Journal of Comparative Law* 6:61–74.

Geertz, Clifford. 1980. *Negara: The Theatre State in Nineteenth-Century Bali*. Princeton, NJ: Princeton University Press.

Gillespie, John. 2007. "Rethinking the Role of Judicial Independence in Socialist-Transforming East Asia." *The International and Comparative Law Quarterly* 56 (4):837–869.

Ginsburg, Tom. 2003. *Judicial Review in New Democracies: Constitutional Courts in Asian Cases*. Cambridge: Cambridge University Press.

Ginsburg, Tom. 2014. "Constitutional Courts in East Asia." In *Comparative Constitutional Law in Asia*, edited by Rosalind Dixon, and Tom Ginsburg, 47–79. Cheltenham: Edward Elgar.

Ginsburg, Tom, and Albert H. Y. Chen, eds. 2009. *Administrative Law and Governance in Asia: Comparative Perspectives*. New York: Routledge.

Ginsburg, Tom, and Nuno Garoupa. 2015. *Judicial Reputation: A Comparative Theory*. Chicago: University of Chicago Press.

Ginsburg, Tom, and Tamir Moustafa, eds. 2008. *Rule of Law: The Politics of Courts in Authoritarian Regimes*. New York: Cambridge University Press.

Gomez, Manuel A. 2009. "Knowledge and Social Networks in the Construction of Elite Lawyers in Venezuela." *Sociologica del Dirritto* 23:113–135.

Granovetter, Mark. 1973. "The Strength of Weak Ties." *American Journal of Sociology* 78 (6):1360–1380.

Haberkorn, Tyrell. 2021. "Under and beyond the Law: Monarchy, Violence, and History in Thailand." *Politics & Society* 49 (3):311–336.

Haggard, Stephan, Andrew MacIntyre, and Lydia Tiede. 2008. "The Rule of Law and Economic Development." *Annual Review of Political Science* 11 (1):205–234.

Hall, Daniel George Edward. 1981. *A History of Southeast Asia*. London: The Macmillan Press.

Halliday, Terence C., Lucien Karpik, and Malcom M. Feeley, eds. 2014. *Fates of Political Liberalism in the British Post-colony: The Politics of the Legal Complex*. Cambridge: Cambridge University Press.

Hammergren, Linn A. 2007. *Envisioning Reform: Improving Judicial Performance in Latin America*. College Park: Pennsylvania State University Press.

Harding, Andrew James. 2016. "Does the 'Basic Structure Doctrine' Apply in Singapore's Constitution? An Inquiry into Some Fundamental Constitutional Premises." In *Constitutional Interpretation in Singapore: Theory and practice*, edited by Jaclyn L. Neo, 32–49. London: Routledge.

Harding, Andrew James. 2001. "Comparative Law and Legal Transplantation in Southeast Asia: Making Sense of the 'Nomic Din'." In *Adapting Legal Culture*, edited by David Nelken, and Rosemary Hunter, 201–222. London: Hart.

Harding, Andrew James. 2010. "The Constitutional Court of Thailand 1998–2006: A Turbulent Innovation." In *New Courts in Asia*, edited by Andrew James Harding, and Penelope Nicholson, 121–144., New York: Routledge.

Harding, Andrew James. 2015. "Legal Traditions of Southeast Asia." In *International Encyclopedia of Social and Behavioural Sciences*, edited by James Wright, 813–818. Oxford: Elsevier.

Harding, Andrew James, and Amanda Whiting. 2012. "Custodian of Civil Liberties and Justice in Malaysia." In *Fates of Political Liberalism in the British Post-colony: The Politics of the Legal Complex*, edited by Terence C. Halliday, Lucien Karpik, and Malcom M. Feeley, 247–304. Oxford: Oxford University Press.

Harding, Andrew James, and Penelope Nicholson. 2010. *New Courts in Asia*. New York: Routledge.

Harlow, Carol, and Richard Rawlings. 2007. "Promoting Accountability in Multilevel Governance: A Network Approach." *European Law Journal* 13 (4):542–562.

Hazelton L. W., Morgan, Rachael K. Hinkle, and Michael J. Nelson. 2023. *The Elevator Effect: Contact and Collegiality in the American Judiciary*. New York: Oxford University Press.

Helmke, Gretchen, and Stephen Levitsky. 2004. "Informal Institutions and Comparative Politics: A Research Agenda." *Perspectives on Politics* 2 (4):725–740.

Helmke, Gretchen, and Steven Levistky. 2006. *Informal Institutions and Democracy: Lessons from Latin America*. Baltimore: Johns Hopkins University Press.

Hendrianto, Stefanus. 2018. *Law and Politics of Constitutional Courts: Indonesia and the Search for Judicial Heroes*. New York: Routledge.

Hilbink, Lisa. 2007. *Judges beyond Politics in Democracy and Dictatorship: Lessons from Chile*. Cambridge: Cambridge University Press.

Hilbink, Lisa. 2008. "Assessing the New Constitutionalism." *Comparative Politics* 40 (2):227–245.

Hilbink, Lisa, and Patricia J. Woods. 2009. "Comparative Sources of Judicial Empowerment: Ideas and Interests." *Political Research Quarterly* 62 (4): 745–752.

Hill, Clauspeter, and Joerg Menzel, eds. 2009. *Constitutionalism in Southeast Asia* Vol. 1: National Constitutions/ASEAN Charter. Singapore: Konrad Adenauer Foundation.

Hirschl, Ran. 2004. *Towards Juristocracy: The Origins and Consequences of the New Constitutionalism*. Cambridge, MA: Harvard University Press.

Hirschl, Ran. 2006. "The New Constitutionalism and the Judicialization of Pure Politics Worldwide." *Fordham Law Review* 75:721–754.

Hirschl, Ran. 2008a. "The Judicialization of Mega-Politics and the Rise of Political Courts." *Annual Review of Political Science* 11:93–118.

Hirschl, Ran. 2008b. "The Judicialization of Politics." In *The Oxford Handbook of Law and Politics*, edited by Keith E. Whittington, Daniel R. Kelemen, and Gregory A. Caldeira, 119–141. New York: Oxford University Press.

Hooker, Michael Barry. 1978. *A Concise Legal History of South-East Asia*. Oxford: Clarendon Press.

Horowitz, Donald. 2013. *Constitutional Change and Democracy in Indonesia*. Cambridge: Cambridge University Press.

Hurst, William. 2020. *Ruling before the Law: The Politics of Legal Regimes in China and Indonesia*. Cambridge: Cambridge University Press.

Hutchcroft, Paul D. 1998. *Booty Capitalism: The Politics of Banking in the Philippines*. Ithaca: Cornell University Press.

Hutchcroft, Paul D. 2017. "The Politics of Privilege: Rents and Corruption in Asia." In *Political Corruption*, edited by Arnold J. Heidenheimer, and Michael Johnston, 489–513. New York: Routledge.

Ingram, Matthew C. 2016a. *Crafting Courts in New Democracies: The Politics of Subnational Judicial Reform in Brazil and Mexico*. Cambridge: Cambridge University Press.

Ingram, Matthew C. 2016b. "Networked Justice: Judges, the Diffusion of Ideas, and Legal Reform Movements in Mexico." *Journal of Latin American Studies* 48 (4):739–768.

International Bar Association. 2008. *Prosperity versus Individual Rights? Human Rights, Democracy and Rule of Law in Singapore*. London.

International Bar Association. 2015. *Justice versus Corruption Challenges to the Independence of the Judiciary in Cambodia*. London.

Jacobs, Norman. 1971. *Modernizing without Development: Thailand as an Indonesian Case Study*. New York: Praeger.

Jayasuriya, Kanishka. 1999. "Corporatism and Judicial Independence with Statist Legal Institutions in East Asia." In *Law, Capitalism and Power in Asia: The Rule of Law and Legal Institutions*, edited by Kanishka Jayasuriya, 147–173. London: Routledge.

Johnson, Aaron Micah. 2016. "The Judicialization of Politics: An Examination of the Administrative Court of Thailand." DeKalb: Department of Political Science, Northern Illinois University.

Juwana, Hikmahanto. 2014. "Courts in Indonesia: A Mix of Western and Local Character." In *Asian Courts in Context*, edited by Jiunn-rong Yeh, and Wen Chen Chang, 303–339. Cambridge: Cambridge University Press.

Kanagasabai, Chandra. 2012. "Malaysia: Limited and Intermittent Judicialization of Politics." In *The Judicialization of Politics in Asia*, edited by Björn Dressel, 202–218., New York: Routledge Curzon, forthcoming.

Kapiszewski, Diana. 2011. "Tactical Balancing: High Court Decision Making on Politically Crucial Cases." *Law and Society Review* 45 (2):471–506.

Kapiszewski, Diana, Gordon Silverstein, and Robert A. Kagan, eds. 2013a. *Consequential Courts: Judicial Roles in Global Perspective*. Cambridge: Cambridge University Press.

Kapiszewski, Diana, Gordon Silverstein, and Robert A. Kagan. 2013b. "Expanding Judicial Roles in New or Restored Democracies." In *Consequential Courts*, edited by Diana Kapiszewski, Gordon Silverstein, and Robert A. Kagan, 1–44. Cambridge: Cambridge University Press.

Katz, Daniel M., and Derek K. Stafford. 2010. "Hustle and Flow: A Social Network Analysis of the American Federal Judiciary." *Ohio State Law Journal* 71 (3):467–510.

Keong, Chan Sek. 2010. "Judicial Review – From Angst to Empathy." *Singapore Academy of Law Journal* 22:469–489.

Khoo, Boo Teik. 1999. "Between Law and Politics: The Malaysian Judiciary since Independence." In *Law, Capitalism and Power in Asia*, edited by Kanishka Jayasuriya, 205–232. London: Routledge.

Kiernan, Ben. 2008. *The Pol Pot Regime: Race, Power, and Genocide in Cambodia under the Khmer Rouge, 1975–79*. New Haven: Yale University Press.

Klein, James R. 2003. "The Battle for the Rule of Law in Thailand: The Constitutional Court of Thailand." In *The Constitutional Court of Thailand: The Provisions and the Working of the Court*, edited by Amara Raksasataya, and James R Klein, 34–90. Bangkok: Constitution for the People Society.

Krygier, Martin. 2016. "The Rule of Law: Pasts, Presents, and Two Possible Futures." *Annual Review of Law and Social Science* 12 (1):199–229.

Lande, Carl. 1983. "Political Clientelism in Political Studies: Retrospect and Prospects." *International Political Science Review* 4 (4):435–454.

Lee, Hoong Phun, and Marilyn Pittard. 2017a. "Asia-Pacific Judiciaries." In *Asia-Pacific Judiciaries: Independence, Impartiality and Integrity*, edited by H. P. Lee, and Marilyn Pittard, 1–8. Cambridge: Cambridge University Press.

Lee, Hoong Phun, and Marylin Pittard. 2017b. *Asia-Pacific Judiciaries: Independence, Impartiality and Integrity*. Cambridge: Cambridge University Press.

Lee, Hoong Phun, and Richard S. K. Foo. 2017. "The Malaysian Judiciary: A Sisyphean Quest for Redemption." In *Asia-Pacific Judiciaries: Independence, Impartiality and Integrity*, edited by Hoong Phun Lee, and Marilyn Pittard, 231–263. Cambridge: Cambridge University Press.

Lee, Hoong Phun. 1995. *Constitutional Conflicts in Contemporary Malaysia*. New York: Oxford University Press.

Leiter, Brian. 2010. "Legal Formalism and Legal Realism: What Is the Issue?" *Legal Theory* 16 (2):111–133.

Lev, Daniel S. 1996. "Between State and Society: Professional Lawyers and Reform in Indonesia." In *Making Indonesia: Essays on Modern Indonesia in Honor of George McT. Kahin*, edited by Daniel S. Lev, and Ruth McVey, 144–163. Ithaca: Southeast Asia Program, Cornell University.

Leyland, Peter. 2008. "Thailand's Constitutional Watchdogs: Dobermans, Bloodhounds or Lapdogs?" *Journal of Comparative Law* 2:151–177.

Li-ann, Thio. 2012. "Between Apology and Apogee, Autochthony: The 'Rule of Law' beyond the Rules of Law in Singapore." *Singapore Journal of Legal Studies*:269–297.

Lin, Chien-Chih. 2017. "Autocracy, Democracy, and Juristocracy: The Wax and Wane of Judicial Power in the Four Asian Tigers." *Georgetown Journal of International Law* 48 (4):1063–1144.

Lin, Jolene. 2009. "The Judicialization of Governance: The Case of Singapore." In *Administrative Law and Governance in Asia: Comparative Perspectives*, edited by Tom Ginsburg, and Albert H. Y. Chen, 287–312. London: Routledge.

Lindsey, Timothy, and Kerstin Steiner. 2012. *Islam, Law and the State in Southeast Asia. Volume III: Malaysia and Brunei*. London: I.B. Tauris.

Littlemore, Stuart. 1998. Report to the International Commission of Jurists Geneva, Switzerland, on a Defamation Trial in the High Court of Singapore, Goh Chok Tong vs J. B. Jeyaratnam August 18–22.

Llanos, Mariana, Cordula Tibi Weber, Charlotte Heyl, and Alexander Stroh. 2014. "Informal Interference in the Judiciary in New Democracies: A Comparison of Six African and Latin American Cases." *Democratization* 23 (7):1236–1253.

Lukito, Ratno. 2012. *Legal Pluralism in Indonesia: Bridging the Unbridgeable*. New York: Routledge.

Mahoney, James, and Kathleen Thelen. 2010. "A Theory of Gradual Institutional Change." In *Explaining Institutional Change: Ambiguity, Agency, and Power*, edited by James Mahoney, and Kathleen Thelen, 1–37. Cambridge: Cambridge University Press.

Malleson, Kate, and Peter H. Russell, eds. 2006. *Appointing Judges in an Age of Judicial Power: Critical Perspectives from around the World*. Toronto: University of Toronto Press.

Marti, Gabriela. 2015. "The Role of the Constitutional Tribunal in Myanmar's Reform Process." *Asian Journal of Comparative Law* 10:153–184.

Massoud, Mark Fathi. 2013. *Law's Fragile State: Colonial, Authoritarian, and Humanitarian Legacies in Sudan*. Cambridge: Cambridge University Press.

Matson, John Nathan. 1993. "The Common Law Abroad: English and Indigenous Laws in the British Commonwealth." *The International and Comparative Law Quarterly* 42 (4):753–779.

McCargo, Duncan. 2020. *Fighting for Virtue: Justice and Politics in Thailand*. Ithaca: Cornell University Press.

Meierhenrich, Jens. 2010. *The Legacies of Law: Long-Run Consequences of Legal Development in South Africa, 1652–2000*. Cambridge: Cambridge University Press.

Mérieau, Eugénie. 2016. "Thailand's Deep State, Royal Power and the Constitutional Court (1997–2015)." *Journal of Contemporary Asia* 46 (3):445–466.

Mietzner, Marcus. 2010. "Political Conflict and Democratic Consolidation in Indonesia: The Role of the Constitutional Court." *Journal of East Asian Studies* 10 (3):397–424.

Mitchell, J. Clyde. 1974. "Social Networks." *Annual Review of Anthropology* 3:279–299.

Moustafa, Tamir. 2018. *Constituting Religion: Islam, Liberal Rights, and the Malaysian State, Cambridge Studies in Law and Society.* Cambridge: Cambridge University Press.

Muno, Wolfgang. 2010. "Conceptualizing and Measuring Clientelism." Paper Presented at the Neopatrimonialism in various World Regions, Hamburg.

Nelson, Michael H. 2006. "Political Turmoil in Thailand: Thaksin, Protests, Elections, and the King." *eastasia.at* 5 (1):1–22.

Neo, Jaclyn L. 2015. "Competing Imperatives: Conflicts and Convergences in State and Islam in Pluralist Malaysia." *Oxford Journal of Law and Religion* 4 (1):1–25.

Neo, Jaclyn L. 2018. "Towards a 'Thin' Basic Structure Doctrine in Singapore." *IConnect Blog*, January 17. www.iconnectblog.com/2018/1/towards-a-thin-basic-structure-doctrine-in-singapore-i-connect-column/.

Neo, Jaclyn N. 2017. *Constitutional Interpretation in Singapore: Theory and Practice.* New York: Routledge.

Nicholson, Penelope. 2007. *Borrowing Court Systems: The Experience of Socialist Vietnam.* Leiden: Martinus Nijhoff.

Ockey, James. 2023. "Democratic Decline and Rising Autocratization in Southeast Asia: An Organizing Framework." In *Democratic Recession, Autocratization, and Democratic Backlash in Southeast Asia*, edited by James Ockey, and Naimah S. Talib, 1–32. Singapore: Springer Nature Singapore.

Osborne, Milton. 2004. *Southeast Asia: An Introductory History.* 9th ed. Crows Nest: Allen & Unwin.

Peerenboom, Randall. 2004. *Asian Discourses of Rule of Law.* London: Routledge Curzon.

Pellegrina Lucia, Dalla, Laarni Escresa, and Nuno Garoupa. 2014. "Measuring Judicial Ideal Points in New Democracies: The Case of the Philippines." *Asian Journal of Law and Society* 1 (1):125–164.

Phongpaichit, Pasuk, and Chris Baker. 2014. *A History of Thailand.* 3rd ed. Cambridge: Cambridge University Press.

Pompe, Sebastiaan. 2005. *The Indonesian Supreme Court: A Study of Institutional Collapse.* Ithaca: Cornell University Press.

Posner, Richard A. 2008. *How Judges Think.* Cambridge, MA: Harvard University Press.

Pruksacholavit, Panthip, and Nuno Garoupa. 2016. "Patterns of Judicial Behavior in the Thai Constitutional Court, 2008–2014: An Empirical Approach." *Asian Pacific Law Review* 24 (1):16–35.

Rajah, Jothie. 2012. *Authoritarian Rule of Law: Legislation, Discourse and Legitimacy in Singapore*. Cambridge: Cambridge University Press.

Rose, Carol. 1998. "The 'New' Law and Development Movement in the Post-Cold War Era: A Vietnam Case Study." *Law & Society Review* 32 (1):93–140.

Rose-Ackerman, Susan, Diane A. Desierto, and Natalia Volosin. 2011. "Hyper-Presidentialism: Separation of Powers without Checks and Balances in Argentina and Philippines." *Berkeley J. Int'l Law* 29 (1):246–333.

Roux, Theunis. 2018a. "Indonesia's Judicial Review Regime in Comparative Perspective." *Constitutional Review* 4 (2):131–164.

Roux, Theunis. 2018b. *The Politico-Legal Dynamics of Judicial Review: A Comparative Analysis, Comparative Constitutional Law and Policy*. Cambridge: Cambridge University Press.

Satayanurug, Pawat, and Nattaporn Nakornin. 2014. "Courts in Thailand: Progressive Development as the Country's Pillar of Justice." In *Asian Courts in Context*, edited by Jiunn-rong Yeh, and Wen-Chen Chang, 407–446. Cambridge: Cambridge University Press.

Scherer, Nancy, and Banks Miller. 2009. "The Federalist Society's Influence on the Federal Judiciary." *Political Research Quarterly* 62 (2):366–378.

Scott, John. 2013. *Social Network Analysis*. London: SAGE.

Scribner, Druscilla. 2004. *Limiting Presidential Power: Supreme Court-Executive Relations in Argentina and Chile*. San Diego: University of California.

Segal, Jeffrey A. 2008. "Judicial Behavior." In *The Oxford Handbook of Law and Politics*, edited by Keith E. Whittington, Daniel R. Kelemen, and Gregory A. Caldeira, 19–34. Oxford: Oxford University Press.

Segal, Jeffrey A., and Harold J. Spaeth. 1993. *The Supreme Court and the Attitudinal Model*. New York: Cambridge University Press.

Segal, Jeffrey A., and Harold J. Spaeth. 2002. *The Supreme Court and the Attitudinal Model Revisited*. Cambridge: Cambridge University Press.

Shah, Dian A. H. 2020. "Malaysia's Game of Thrones amid a Pandemic: Constitutional Implications and Political Significance of the State of Emergency." *International Journal of Constitutional Law Blog*, January 17. www.iconnectblog.com/2021/01/malaysias-game-of-thrones-amid-a-pandemic-constitutional-implications-and-political-significance-of-the-state-of-emergency/.

Shapiro, Martin. 1981. *Courts: A Comparative and Political Analysis*. Chicago: Chicago University Press.

Shapiro, Martin. 1999. "The Success of Judicial Review." In *Constitutional Dialogues in Comparative Perspective*, edited by Sally J. Kenney, William M. Reisinger, and John C. Reitz, 193–219. New York: Palgrave Macmillan.

Shapiro, Martin, and Alec Stone Sweet. 2002. *On Law, Politics, and Judicialization*. New York: Oxford University Press.

Sieder, Rachel. 2010. "Renegotiating 'Law and Order': Judicial Reform and Citizen Responses in Post-war Guatemala." *Democratization* 7 (1):137–160.

Sieder, Rachel, Line Schjolden, and Alan Angell. 2005a. "Introduction." In *The Judicialization of Politics in Latin America*, edited by Rachel Sieder, Line Schjolden, and Alan Angell, 1–21. New York: Palgrave Macmillan.

Sieder, Rachel, Line Schjolden, and Alan Angell, eds. 2005b. *The Judicialization of Politics in Latin America*. New York: Palgrave Macmillan.

Slater, Dan. 2010. *Ordering Power: Contentious Politics and Authoritarian Leviathans in Southeast Asia*. Cambridge: Cambridge University Press.

Slaughter, Anne Marie. 2000. "Judicial Globalization." *Virginia Journal of International Law* 40:1103–1124.

Spiller, Pablo, and Rafael Gely. 2010. "Strategic Judicial Decision-Making." In *The Oxford Handbook of Law and Politics*, edited by Keith E. Whittington, Daniel R. Kelemen, and Gregory A. Caldeira, 35–43. Oxford: Oxford University Press.

Staton, Jeffrey K. 2010. *Judicial Power and Strategic Communication in Mexico*. Cambridge: Cambridge University Press.

Steinberg, David Joel. 1988. *In Search of Southeast Asia: A Modern History*. Revised ed. Honolulu: University of Hawaii Press.

Stephenson, Matthew. 2007. "Judicial Reform in Developing Economies: Constraints and Opportunities." In *Annual World Bank Conference on Development Economics Region: Beyond Transition*, edited by Francois Bourguignon, and Boris Pleskovic, 311–329. Washington, DC: The World Bank.

Stone Sweet, Alec. 2000. *Governing with Judges: Constitutional Politics in Europe*. Oxford: Oxford University Press.

Streckfuss, David. 2011. *Truth on Trial in Thailand: Defamation, Treason, and Lèse-Majesté*. New York: Routledge.

Sunstein, Cass R. 2001. *Designing Democracy. What Constitutions Do*. Oxford: Oxford University Press.

Tamahana, Brian. 2004. *Rule of Law: History, Politics, Theory*. Cambridge: Cambridge University Press.

Tamahana, Brian. 2010. *Beyond the Formalist-Realist Divide*. Princeton: Princeton University Press.

Tan, Kevin Y. L. 2002. "The Making and Remaking of Constitutions in Southeast Asia: An Overview." *Singapore Journal of International & Comparative Law* 6:1–41.

Tan, Kevin Y. L. 2017. "The Singapore Judiciary." In *Asia-Pacific Judiciaries: Independence, Impartiality and Integrity*, edited by Hoong Phun Lee, and Marilyn Pittard, 284–304. Cambridge: Cambridge University Press.

Tate, C. Neal. 1994. "The Judicialization of Politics in the Philippines and Southeast Asia." *International Political Science Review / Revue internationale de science politique* 15 (2):187–197.

Tate, Neal C., and Torbjörn Vallinder, eds. 1995. *The Global Expansion of Judicial Power*. New York: New York University Press.

Taylor, Keith. 1999. "The Early Kingdoms." In *The Cambridge History of Southeast Asia*, edited by Nicholas Tarling, 137–181. Cambridge: Cambridge University Press.

Tew, Yvonne. 2016. "On the Uneven Journey to Constitutional Redemption: The Malaysian Judiciary and Constitutional Politics." *Washington International Law Journal* 25 (3):673–696.

Tew, Yvonne. 2020. *Constitutional Statecraft in Asian Courts*. Oxford: Oxford University Press.

Thio, Li-ann. 2005. "Beyond the Four Walls in an Age of Transnational Judicial Conversations Civil Liberties, Rights Theories, and Constitutional Adjudication in Malaysia and Singapore." *Columbia Journal of Asian Law* 19:430–457.

Thomas, Tommy. 1987. "The Role of the Judiciary." *Aliran* (Reflections on the Malaysian Constitution):54–108.

Thomas, Tommy. 2021. *My Story: Justice in the Wilderness*. Kuala Lumpur: Strategic Research and Development Centre.

Thompson, Virginia. 1937. *French Indo-China*. London: George Allen & Unwin.

Tilly, Charles, ed. 1975. *The Formation of National States in Western Europe*. Princeton: Princeton University Press.

Tonsakulrungruang, Khemthong. 2016. "Thailand: An Abuse of Judicial Review." In *Judicial Review of Elections in Asia*, edited by Po Jen Yap, 173–192. New York: Routledge.

Tonsakulrungruang, Khemthong. 2017. "Entrenching the Minority: The Constitutional Court in Thailand's Political Conflict." *Washington Law Review* 26 (2):247–267.

Tonsakulrungruang, Khemthong. 2022. "Thailand." In *2021 Global Review of Constitutional Law*, edited by Richard Albert, David Landau, Pietro Faraguna, Simon Drugda, and Rocio De Carolis, 348–352. Austin: University of Texas.

Trochev, Alexei, and Rachel Ellett. 2014. "Judges and Their Allies." *Journal of Law and Courts* 2 (1):67–91.

Trowell, Mark. 2015. *The Prosecution of Anwar Ibrahim: The Final Play.* Singapore: Marshall Cavendish.

van Tai, Tan. 1982. "Vietnam's Code of the Lê Dynasty (1428–1788), 30 AM. J. COMP. L. 523, 523–25." *American Journal of Comparative Law* 30 (3):523–554.

Vitug, Martites Danguilan. 2010. *Shadow of Doubt: Probing the Supreme Court.* Quezon City: Public Trust Media Group.

Vitug, Martites Danguilan. 2012. *Hour before Dawn: The Fall and Uncertain Rise of the Philippine Supreme Court.* Quezon City: Cleverheads.

Weiss, Meredith L. 2006. *Protest and Possibilities: Civil Society and Coalitions for Political Change in Malaysia.* Palo Alto: Stanford University Press.

West, Lucy. 2019. "The limits to Judicial Independence: Cambodia's Political Culture and the Civil Law." *Democratization* 26 (3):537–553.

Whittington, Keith E. 2000. "Once More unto the Breach: Post-behavioralist Approaches to Judicial Politics." *Law and Social Inquiry* 25 (3):601–634.

Winters, Jeffrey A. 2012. "Oligarchs and Oligarchy in Southeast Asia." In *Routledge Handbook of Southeast Asian Politics*, edited by Richard Robison, 53–82. London: Routledge.

Wolters, Oliver William. 1999. *History, Culture, and Region in Southeast Asian Perspectives.* Revised ed. Ithaca: Cornell University Southeast Asia Program, and Institute of Southeast Asian Studies.

World Bank. 2003. *Legal and Judicial Reform: Strategic Directions.* Washington, DC: The World Bank.

Worthington, Ross. 2001. "Between Hermes and Themis: An Empirical Study of the Contemporary Judiciary in Singapore." *Journal of Law and Society* 28 (4):490–519.

Worthington, Ross. 2003. *Governance in Singapore.* London: Routledge Curzon.

Yap, Po Jen. 2017. *Courts and Democracies in Asia.* Cambridge: Cambridge University Press.

Cambridge Elements ≡

Politics and Society in Southeast Asia

Edward Aspinall

Australian National University

Edward Aspinall is a professor of politics at the Coral Bell School of Asia-Pacific Affairs, Australian National University. A specialist of Southeast Asia, especially Indonesia, much of his research has focused on democratisation, ethnic politics and civil society in Indonesia and, most recently, clientelism across Southeast Asia.

Meredith L. Weiss

University at Albany, SUNY

Meredith L. Weiss is Professor of Political Science at the University at Albany, SUNY. Her research addresses political mobilization and contention, the politics of identity and development, and electoral politics in Southeast Asia, with particular focus on Malaysia and Singapore.

About the Series

The Elements series Politics and Society in Southeast Asia includes both country-specific and thematic studies on one of the world's most dynamic regions. Each title, written by a leading scholar of that country or theme, combines a succinct, comprehensive, up-to-date overview of debates in the scholarly literature with original analysis and a clear argument.

Milton Keynes UK
Ingram Content Group UK Ltd.
UKHW051907270324
440086UK00021B/188